KU-474-920

THE ART

OF

MANAGING

Bill Scott and Sven Söderberg

Wildwood House

© Bill Scott and Sven Söderberg 1985

All rights reserved. No part of this publication may be reproduced, stored in a retrieval system, or transmitted in any form or by any means, electronic, mechanical, photocopying, recording, or otherwise without the prior permission of Wildwood House Limited.

First published in Great Britain in hardback by Gower Publishing Company Limited, 1985

This paperback edition published in Great Britain in 1986 by
Wildwood House Limited,
Gower House,
Croft Road,
Aldershot,
Hampshire GU11 3HR,
England

Reprinted 1988, 1989

British Library Cataloguing in Publication Data

Scott, Bill, *1925–*
    The art of managing.
    1. Management
    I. Title   II. Söderberg, Sven
    658.4   HD31

ISBN 0-7045-0525-8

Typeset by Graphic Studios (Southern) Limited
Godalming, Surrey
Printed and bound in Great Britain by
Biddles Limited, Guildford and King's Lynn

Dedication: J. & B.

14046 BIFCSE

BELFAST PUBLIC LIBRARIES

THE ART OF MANAGING

BELFAST PUBLIC LIBRARIES

DATE DUE	DATE DUE	DATE DUE

APPLICATION FOR RENEWAL MAY

BE MADE IN PERSON, BY WRITING

OR BY TELEPHONE.

CL3

Contents

PART 2 Results: The Art of Managing for Results

PART 3 Ability to Achieve: Taking up Position

PART 4 Direction: Heading in the Right Direction

Acknowledgements

For their help in the conception and development of this book:

    Stella Ascott JP
    Malcolm Stern.

For their stimuli to our thinking and to our careers, a host of our manager-friends.

The extent to which our thinking has been influenced by the writing of other people is acknowledged in the appendix.

This book is full of examples. With only minor exceptions these examples are taken from real life; but to preserve anonymity, names have been changed and situations sufficiently camouflaged.

What this book is about

This is a book for practical managers.

It is a book of suggestions, ideas, tips, which have been found to be helpful by our many friends who are themselves managers.

They are people who have much in common. They work intensely. They are devoted to the interests of their organisations and of their people. They strive to cope with changing conditions and with all the limitations imposed on them by the organisation and other people in it, and by the outside business world and the government. They get a fair amount of satisfaction, but are rarely satisfied.

They have much in common but there are many differences between them. Their jobs range in size from managing directors of massive organisations to managers in charge of relatively small departments. They include people managing in all sizes of organisation, big, small, even one-man bands; and in all types of organisation – industrial, engineering, commercial, public service. They include people involved in marketing, in manufacturing, and in financing, banking, insurance; and specialist supporters, personnel, accounting, technical. And they include professionals – engineers, scientists, lawyers, economists.

They are different people in different organisations under different pressures. Each is an individual. Each has his own character, competence, zeal, strengths; each his own hopes and drives and values. Each practises the art of managing in his own way.

Working in their different ways, most managers of our acquaintance are well on top of their jobs, and at the same time they share a common urge to be better at it. They are people who achieve a great deal and are tolerably satisfied. Only "tolerably", because the satisfaction is constantly offset by a sense of inadequacy, a concern to do better, an anxiety to develop the art.

This "divine discontent" is both a blessing and a curse. Without it, we would lose our sparkle and our ambition, but it must be kept constantly balanced with a reasonable degree of satisfaction. Keeping that balance is in itself an art of the competent manager.

So is another sort of "balancing": the balance between enjoying oneself, getting results, earning a position which will enable us to achieve even better results, and making sure that those results will be to the profit of our employers, our own staff and ourselves.

These are all legitimate management activities. All must be kept in some sort of balance, and this book contains ideas and techniques to help you keep a good balance and to develop the art of managing.

The shape of the book

The underlying idea is that managers have constantly to balance their work in four distinct areas. This is a balancing act which is being constantly undertaken, not always consciously, but always under the real pressures of daily life and one's own personality and possibilities.

The book opens with a chapter identifying those four main fields.

The main part of the book is then presented in four parts, one part for each of the main fields.

Within each field there are a variety of "forces", just as there are forces within a magnetic field. The manager has not only to balance the attention he gives to each of the four fields; he must also balance the six or seven forces within each field.

There is a chapter for each force, leading to suggestions for action when any are out of balance.

Within most of these chapters there is a standard sequence; a brief statement of the particular force, some examples of how it works, a review of those examples as object lessons, and, finally, some suggestions for action.

Throughout the central parts of the book we try to help managers to keep a balance among the forces within each of the fields.

In the final chapter, we revert to the theme of keeping a balance among the four main fields.

A note on language

The English language is no help to anyone wanting to do justice to both sexes, and the word "he" throughout the text should usually be taken to stand for "he or she".

Bill Scott	Sven Söderberg
12 Trafalgar Road	Askåkersplan 23
Southport	Askim
England	Sweden

1 The Balancing Act

Managers are constantly under pressure. They have to keep control of events and to take initiatives. They have to satisfy the needs of their organisations and the expectations of their colleagues and their customers. They are surrounded by rules and regulations, formal and informal. They need to satisfy all they can of the requirements of this surrounding world.

And they need to satisfy themselves. Unless they find genuine enjoyment from their activities as managers, they will not be happy and satisfied in their work.

Their scope for modifying the ways in which they work is severely limited. Too much is determined by history and by circumstances beyond their own control. Nevertheless, their satisfaction and success in managing depend on their ability to influence events.

That influence must balance a whole range of forces. Unless they manage to keep a balance, they and their organisations will cease to be satisfied with one another. Let us consider a few examples.

Examples

John Goldman was a senior personnel officer, right at the top of middle management in a large paper-making group. He was happy, always had a smile and a cheerful word for his colleagues. As a senior specialist he had to advise numerous departments in factories all over the country and abroad. His "customers" respected him, and he was able to inspire them and help them to improve their performance.

He manoeuvred so that he became attached to an authoritative figure in his group, who was able to create conditions in which John's talents were readily seen, recognised and used by the departments. The strategy to which he worked was agreed between himself, his boss and the heads of various departments.

All went well. John drove happily and quickly to work each morning, left late each evening and drove home happily – though less quickly – to a secure and welcoming family.

One day, however, things changed. New owners took over, John's boss moved to another organisation, the new boss did not respect the same values, John was no longer able to achieve the same results.

What to do? John worked hard to influence the new boss and to bring all the pressures he could to bear, but the new boss had no respect for what John had been trying to do.

After four months, John realised that he now drove to work more slowly than he drove home in the evenings.

John left.

Jim Rushton was a marketing manager, an expert with people. He was ever friendly and courteous. He was popular both within his company and with the customers. He enjoyed his work and was constantly able to manoeuvre himself, perhaps unconsciously, into positions in which he was welcome and in which, increasingly, he could influence the company's activities. He had plenty of contacts who could suggest suitable directions in which to develop the organisation.

He enjoyed his work, his colleagues benefited from the way he lubricated the communications within the organisation: the organisation prospered. Jim moved to higher and higher responsibility.

Until suddenly the organisation was no longer making a profit. Then the searchlights were turned on inside the company and people began to worry about performance.

In fact, Jim had been so superb at enjoying himself, helping others to enjoy themselves, swimming with the tide, that neither he nor anybody else had recognised that his department had produced zero result.

There was only one thing for it. Jim had to go.

Eileen Berry was a very mature young lady. She worked very hard and had a personality which drew the support of colleagues old and young. She was able to agree with her bosses on the strategies which she should follow, both to enjoy herself and to get results.

In a series of appointments with her company, Eileen for several years sustained her satisfaction and her success-rate.

Yet somehow her career did not blossom at the rate her success would seem to merit. It was not because of any lack of competence, lack of effort or direction. It was simply that she never managed to get into a position in which she was properly protected and developed by someone in top authority.

Over the years Eileen remained trapped in roles well below her potential level of ability.

Harry Green was the sort of young man who just missed going to university. He joined a watchmaking company and quickly became expert in watch mechanisms.

Working in a company which did not have too many
bright lights in it, he was seen to be of exceptional calibre
and was promoted to be technical director of his
company at a very young age. He worked hard and
enjoyably to sustain and develop the company's products, and had special success with a small high-quality
ladies' watch. Indeed, when he first heard of the
possibility of quartz clocks and watches, Harry worked
even harder to perfect his ladies' watch. It was sad that
the market for conventional watches had vanished
before he succeeded.

Analysis

The four examples above have been chosen to represent
managerial problems of four different sorts.

In the first field there was John Goldman. John enjoyed
himself and had Fun; he obtained Results; he had the
Ability to Achieve; and the Direction of his effort was
positive.

His working life had four ingredients:

● *Fun*
● *Results*
● *Ability to Achieve*
● *Direction*

As long as he could keep those FRAD fields in balance,
he was a satisfied and successful manager.

When circumstances changed and he found himself
hurrying to leave work, when he found it impossible to
make it Fun, he took the sensible step of quitting.

Jim Rushton's imbalance was different. He was the man
who enjoyed himself, took the right positions, was even
able to go in the right direction, but never obtained any
results. His FRAD pattern was positive on Fun, on taking
positions where he had the Ability to Achieve, and even
in the Direction he went in.

But where Jim missed out was on Results.

Eileen Berry had more ability in that line but never managed to reach a position where she could Achieve all she was capable of.

Harry Green, who enjoyed life and early became technical director, lost out suddenly when there was no demand for his products. He was positive on Fun, positive on Results, positive on Ability to Achieve, but negative on Direction.

This analysis identifies four fields which the successful and satisfied manager must keep in balance. They are:

● Fun : the sheer pleasure of managing.
● Results : the production of positive results.
● Ability to Achieve : reaching a position where one has the resources and the relationships necessary for success.
● Direction : ensuring that one's activities are heading in a profitable direction.

These are important fields which have to be kept in balance. They are the sort of fields each manager needs to review occasionally – maybe once a year.

He needs to ask himself:

● Am I having Fun: am I enjoying it?
● Am I obtaining Results?
● Am I moving into the right position to have Fun and get Results in the future?
● Am I taking my job in the right Direction?
● Is the balance amongst those fields satisfactory?
● What sort of changes should I make to improve the balance?

These are the sort of questions which most of us can pose for ourselves, but not the sort of questions which we find it easy to answer. They are the sort of issues where we are greatly helped if we have a trusted friend, colleague, or adviser, who will act as a speaking partner. One who is prepared to listen to us and to help us to sort out our own ideas without trying to impose on us his own values and answers.

We need to think out the balance among those four

major fields. Within each there are active forces which we shall be looking at in more depth in the four main parts of this book.

Action Dos and Don'ts

DO
- Keep a balance between Fun, Results, Ability to Achieve, and Direction.
- Occasionally take stock of that balance.
- Use a trusted friend or adviser to help you take stock.
- Decide which field merits your priority attention.

DON'T
- Let the four fields become badly unbalanced.
- Postpone your review indefinitely.
- Make a fetish of it. Don't become too engrossed in looking at the grand strategy picture of your job.

DO
- Take stock once a year.

Part 1

THE ART OF ENJOYING MANAGING

INTRODUCTION TO PART 1

A close friend of one of the authors includes in his principles for heading his highly successful company: "If I cannot give anything else as Managing Director of this company, I will see to it that every person in my organisation gets at least one good laugh a day."

Part 1 of this book is about enjoying the job of managing. Without that essential enjoyment, the task of managing is laborious, non-satisfying. The competent manager therefore takes what steps he can towards making it enjoyable.

Different managers enjoy different things, of course, and each must satisfy his own particular sense of enjoyment.

In striving to get the balance right he will need to pay attention to a series of forces. Here are the ones we believe to be the most important:

- His own urge to get on with the job.
- His relations with friends, allies, and enemies.
- The style in which he manages.
- The relation between job and private life.

We devote a chapter to each of these forces, and to the actions the manager can take within each to get the best balance of enjoyment from his job.

2 Having the Urge

Enjoying management is one ingredient of being success-ful at it; but that which is enjoyable is a personal matter. Different people enjoy different things.

There are two ways in which you can influence the chance that you will enjoy your own managing.

First, the fact that you enjoy this or that, depends on you. It depends in part on some characteristics deter-mined before you were born, and on all your experi-ences between then and now. It depends on your childhood experience and on your working experience since you completed your education. These things have moulded you to be what you are.

That is history. You cannot do much about it. But it does help us to enjoy ourselves (and to deal with other people) if we can realise what makes each of us distinctive.

An easy way of recognising personal distinctiveness is to recognise what sort of satisfaction we want from our jobs. Such satisfaction can come in three ways:

- Satisfying *achievement*
  Some people have a great urge to get to grips with a job, to bring it to a successful conclusion. Other people have less urge to achieve.
- Satisfying *affiliation*
  For some, the most important urge is to be with other people, to be in close touch with them, preferably in a way which affects their welfare.
- Satisfying *power*
  Some seek above all for the power to influence events. They long for power, authority, influence, status.

Each of us has his own blend of need for achievement, for affiliation, for power. Your particular blend is something that is deep in you. Equally, each of your colleagues has his own distinctive blend, deep inside him.

Managing is more enjoyable when we recognise and try to satisfy our distinctive wants – and theirs.

Second, we may not be able significantly to change what we are, but we can change what we expect. We each have some sense of what we expect from the next phase of our work. If we achieve what we expect, or nearly achieve it, we are content.

We feel unhappy if our expectations are grossly unsatisfied, *or* if they are grossly *over*satisfied. If you don't gain what you want at all, you'll be dissatisfied; but you can have too much of a good thing. Your expectations depend on your ability to set yourself challenging targets which you can just achieve.

Other people's satisfaction with you also depends on their expectations of you. If you give them too low an expectation, they won't esteem you. If you give them too high an expectation, they will later be dissatisfied.

It's all a matter of balance.

Examples

Peter Jones ran a small merchandising company. He had a staff of about 130, mainly in the warehouse. His success depended on the keenness of his buying and of his selling. He was good at it himself, had a couple of young salesmen to back him. He became grossly overworked, however, and decided that the answer to the problem was to take on a senior salesman, for whom he created the title Sales Director.

Paul Innes was the outstanding candidate for this appointment.

At interview, Peter (the boss) told Paul (the candidate) about the company's growth, painted a rosy picture of its past and continuing success, and gave expectations of a job in which Paul would deal with directors of large stores and with wholesalers.

Paul had plenty of sales management experience but he magnified his limited knowledge of the merchandise. To be honest, he knew little about it, but he felt it important to magnify that little so that he might secure this interesting job.

Within weeks of Paul taking up the job, both parties were dissatisfied. Paul found that his contacts with important customers were oases in a desert of monotonous office-bound routine. Peter found that Paul's knowledge of the merchandise was so limited that he could not feed back important information about the market and the product requirements.

The appointment was a failure. Both Peter and Paul were frustrated.

Arthur Brown was the manager of a highly successful factory, and his great urge was to have influence on the world around him. He gladly accepted a move from his factory to a role as assistant to a director of his company – a role in which he soon found that his influence was minimal. Unhappy in this position, he changed jobs, moved to another company and another corridor of power, in which again he had little influence. Then he moved on to a role in a government enterprise in which, because of his management experience, he was able to influence the distribution of government funds. He found it boring – there was not much activity in which to make use of his managerial talents – but at last his concern to influence events was being satisfied and he put up with the boredom.

George Reid, on the other hand, was a tremendous achiever and inspirer. He had no aspiration to power. He was humble to the point that he needed reassurance before he would accept any promotions. Nevertheless, all around saw him, to his astonishment, as a powerful figure.

His concern for power was so low that he took no steps to prevent the more power-hungry of his colleagues from conspiring against him. People with lesser achievement-records managed then to supplant him.

Yet another type was *Herbert Johnson*. Herbert was dedicated to the importance of his own accountancy discipline. He built around himself a core of ambitious young accountants, manoeuvred himself and his young men increasingly on to influential committees, took tighter and tighter hold on the reins of power. So with dedication and with manipulation, Herbert moved inside his group from cashier to accountant to chief accountant, then to finance director and ultimately to managing director; and, incidentally, he made the group the most successful within its industry.

Frank Woodhead was the successful technical manager of his company. He found that his scientific mind was exercised by the role. His concern to innovate found a good outlet, his relations with his colleagues were good: he was satisfied by the job. Then came talk of a merger.

At first everybody shrugged it off, but it became more and more probable. His colleagues started to worry.

Frank knew that the potential "partner" had a large technical department which had done little but sustain the competitor's established quality, so Frank looked forward to a new innovating role.

But once the merger had taken place, Frank found that the new people in charge, people from the non-innovating competitor, did not appreciate his ability to develop new products. He found it difficult to talk to them. His security was undermined, his ability to be effective was lost. But unlike many of his former colleagues, Frank did not leave, he stayed on, trying to find useful work to do. He lost the urge, the enjoyment of management. Visibly he shrank and aged.

Magnus Hillberg was the highly successful personnel manager in a plant with about 5,000 blue-collar workers. The organisation was highly bureaucratic and everything was done by the rule-book. Despite his success and eminent position in this big company, Magnus found himself frustrated, unable to change the existing situation. He was plainly bored, and he took the plunge and changed jobs.

He moved to the post of personnel manager in a much smaller company (500 employees). Suddenly he found a whole new range of problems and of opportunities to be creative; he was full of enthusiasm.

It didn't last. A year later, Magnus was to be found sitting in his office, gazing vacantly into space. "I am deeply disappointed", he sighed. "The Managing Director just doesn't care enough for personnel problems. There's so much to be done and so little chance to do it. I guess I'll just have to go. Know any good jobs around?"

A year later, Magnus was still in the same job but now revitalised, "in traffic" with the Board, achieving. The secret lay in his use of the ideas in this chapter.

Analysis

Paul Innes did not make a good sales director in Peter Jones's firm. Much of the reason goes back to the false expectations which each gave the other at the first interview.

If Peter had warned Paul of how much routine would be demanded in the job, if Peter had not given ill-founded expectations of the challenges and opportunities, if Peter had at the outset presented the frustrations as challenges to be overcome – then Paul would not have been so frustrated.

If, in his turn, Paul had made clear the limits of his knowledge of the trade, then Peter might have had the wit to ensure some reasonable training programme.

True, of course, that if each had given more reasonable expectations, Paul might not have become a member of the company. But better that than a capable executive so frustrated and quickly leaving with his reputation besmirched; and with the company needing all over again to start the time-consuming business of recruitment, selection and induction.

Reasonable expectations which can largely, if not wholly, be satisfied are an important ingredient of each manager's urge to work.

Each too has his own blend of needs for achievement, for affiliation, for power. Arthur Brown's desire for power was finally met when he moved from a manager's job into government-based corridors of power. His power need was strong enough to overcome the boredom: his need for achievement was not so high.

George Reid on the other hand, high in his need for achievement and affiliation but low in his need for power, had his position usurped by more power-hungry, if less competent people.

Herbert Johnson had driving commitment both for achievement and for power. His need for affiliation was lower, so that he was able to ignore some animosity from his colleagues as he drove for higher and higher influence within his organisation.

Frank Woodhead's circumstances changed radically. He lost the urge to work, lost his ability to be effective, vegetated and withered.

Magnus Hillberg is a very unusual person. He has a fair drive for achievement, a great longing for affiliation, and a strong wish for power. It is rare to find someone whose urges are so strong in all three directions, and such rare people are often full of anxiety. No easy-going devil-may-care attitudes for them, but pent-up concern to achieve, to belong, to influence.

It is our view that he was quite right to leave the large company where he was so frustrated. There was never a chance that he could enjoy managing there.

His new job, he thought, was proving unhappy because the managing director wouldn't listen to him. Seen from the managing director's viewpoint, Magnus had earlier come to him with some interesting ideas, but as soon as he started asking questions about them, Magnus started backing down. (He was scared that he'd lose his ability to gain friendship and influence if he stuck too hard to his fresh ideas.) Faced with such apparent uncertainty, the managing director wondered whether he really could trust this new man's ideas. The seeds of suspicion were soon sown, and within twelve months Magnus was sitting at his desk, glassy-eyed.

But within another 12 months, Magnus was revitalised and successful in the same company. He started that twelve months (with a little outside help) with an effort to teach the managing director and his senior colleagues about his expertise and about the sort of things he should be able to do for them. He created fresh expectations, and he was asked to do one or two secondary things; then suddenly there was a need for some difficult negotiation with the work-force representatives. This was one thing Magnus really was good at. With success in that, soon followed by a couple of highly esteemed management development programmes designed by his department, Magnus was back in business.

Each of the people in these examples had:

- His own blend of motives towards achievement, affiliation and power.
- His own expectations of the future.
- Colleagues' expectations of him, which he had helped to create.

For each, satisfaction and enjoyment depended on striking the right balance.

Action Dos and Don'ts

DO
- Recognise your own individual character. Which do you most value – achievement, affiliation or power? Which least value?
- Try to develop your job so that it will best satisfy that character.
- If your job situation changes (a merger, for example), stand up for what you value. Persevere. But as soon as you realise that it has changed, decide how long you are prepared so to persevere.
- Set your expectations in order. Strike a sound balance between over-optimism and rank pessimism. (If you need help on this, you'll find tips when you come to Part 4 of this book.)
- Help your colleagues to form sensible expectations about what you can do.

DON'T
- Try to imitate your colleagues. Do recognise that they have different urges and needs.
- Give in too soon.
- Persevere too long.

DO
- Concentrate on satisfying yourself.

3 Friends, Allies and Enemies

Every manager is surrounded by people: bosses, colleagues, subordinates, customers, suppliers. . . . They play an important part in his enjoyment (or lack of enjoyment) of his job.

People are of three sorts: friends, allies, enemies.

Friends are essential. They are the sort of people whom we can trust, with whom we can be open, with whom we can easily communicate. We can laugh together, we can share our likes and our dislikes, we can give one another impulses. When we can work together on a project, we can make it sparkle.

Such friendships are precious. They often arise spontaneously, but they always need to be worked on. There can never be complete trust between two people: always there is some element of doubt, however small, in any relationship.

The prudent manager therefore works constantly to earn the benefit of that doubt. He never takes it for granted. He is open and honest with his friends, constantly nurturing their friendship.

Apart from friends, he also has allies. These are people with whom he is able to work, in the interests of getting the job done. Allies are not necessarily friends. They may not share the same jokes, likes, dislikes, but their support is essential.

It behoves the manager to work on his alliances.

Try it for yourself, now. Take a sheet of paper and write on it the name of one ally. Then answer the following questions:

1. What initiatives have I taken to help him recently?
2. What steps have I taken to communicate with him?
3. How frank is the pattern of negotiation between us? Am I doing my utmost?
4. What support have I had from him? What better could I reasonably hope for?
5. What steps can I take now to improve this alliance?

Managers do not have only friends and allies: they inevitably have enemies. "Inevitably", because in any healthy organisation there are bound to be conflicts of opinion and interests which need to be resolved.

But it is not only such "positional" causes which generate enmity. There are in fact three distinct types of enemy.

First, there is the organisationsal enemy. This is the person with whom one needs to take joint action or collaborate in decision-making: or with whom there is some sort of interdependence for support.

Too often we work in organisations which are littered with poor relationships of this organisational sort. There are situations in which the holders of two or three roles all act independently, when the actions of each have significant consequences for the others. They do not realise how interdependent they are.

They have never discussed their respective responsibility, authority, objectives. They see the others as enemies when a little objective discussion can soon show the scope for positive alliance. In this sort of situation some third party is needed to help them overcome the organisational enemy. It's a situation which we consider more fully in Section 7C, "Organising".

Second, there is the positional enemy. It is the advertising manager's job to spend money. It is the comptroller's job to curb that spending. Their positions therefore are in opposition.

But this is no reason why the individuals should constantly be in opposition. They will need constantly to restate their own positions, both privately and publicly, and these will be different positions; but they can work openly with one another and can yet respect the differences between their positions.

The *third* type of enemy is the one with a divergent personality.

Sometimes this personality difference may be overcome. For example, if one is genuinely not ambitious, then one has the possibility of supporting and helping a power-oriented "enemy". One can then win the support of that divergent personality. It is not easy – he will have great difficulty in accepting that others do not have the same driving ambition as he has. Nevertheless, the route to co-operation does exist and the competent manager will find and explore that route. It is fun!

But finally there is always the chance with such a conflict of personality that no co-operation is possible. Recognise such situations. Do not be misled by well intended nonsense about always being open, but try to find positive ways to cope with them.

When trying to work out routes towards overcoming this sort of enmity, it is helpful to think in terms of winning and losing.

There are three possible situations: win–win, win–lose, or lose–lose. In the first situation both parties gain from co-operation. In the second one party is winning and the other losing. In the third situation both parties lose from the "co-operation".

The lose–lose situation is by no means abnormal. It is precisely what happens when two enemies would rather both lose than risk the other party gaining.

The win–lose situation is, however, more common.

The manager sometimes does not recognise that his own results form part of a larger whole. Therefore he works only for his own gain, eventually creating a less profitable result for the whole. The win side of the win–lose situation can be fun, but only until the other party gets the better of you next time.

The win–win situation arises when both parties, be they enemies, allies or friends, find profitable ways to solve a problem or explore an opportunity together. By raising their eyes above the level of the present skirmish, they can creatively find new ways that could profit them both. It needs a dose of "helicopter ability" – the capacity to rise a little above the level of petty skirmishing.

To develop a win–win situation together with an enemy could turn him into an ally.

To develop a win–win situation together with an ally could turn him into a friend.

Each is fun.

To summarise, enmity in organisations has three causes:

- Organisational differences, where managers need to work on the interdependence between the different roles.
- Positional differences, where each manager has to learn respect for the other's job demands.
- Divergent personalities, where the manager has to develop acceptance and respect for the (other) divergent personality and try to find a win–win solution – and maybe develop his "helicopter ability".

Examples

"The trouble with you", she said, "is that they are frightened of you." She was a secretary who had worked for one of us for two years.

"What, me? Rubbish! They have nothing to be frightened of."

"That's not what they think. They see all these ideas

that you keep putting up and they do not really understand them properly. They are frightened of the ideas and they are frightened of you."

And so she went on. Finally she convinced me that she might be right.

"Well, all right then," I said, "what do we do about it?"

"You have got to make more use of your allies", she said. "Take Harry [another member of the department]; he has never had a fraction of your ideas, but nobody could ever be frightened of Harry, he is so meek. He has worked for you for three years now, he trusts you completely and you can trust him. Why don't you get him to go and see them?"

"She" in this dialogue was Joan Playfair. We had worked together for some time and formed a strong partnership. She was always fearless and frank in everything she said to me. A great friend.

Harry was a great ally. He trusted me, we could work together quite well, but somehow we never got round to having quite the same sparkle in our partnership. Nevertheless, the less powerful Harry was largely successful in explaining to other departments.

We had our friends and allies and our enemies in those other departments. Barry, Charles and David were three of the managers we dealt with, and at that time it was our job to give them a technical service. On one occasion we recognised that a new method of testing could provide information more rapidly and more accurately than we had yet been doing. We worked with all three to get their acquiescence. Barry and Charles both readily agreed and gave us their support, but David opposed us. However hard we worked at it, whatever pressures we were able to bring on David, it made no difference. We should have realised more quickly that David was such an enemy that there was no way we were going to convert him. We should not have wasted our time.

Barry and Charles had given us their support and we put the new system in. It had its teething troubles: the print-outs were not clear in the early stages, and one of the programmes proved to be defective; but, nevertheless, with Barry we were able to ensure that he soon came to have a much better service.

Charles on the other hand was soon swayed by some of his subordinates, whose real interests lay in clinging to an obsolete system. We were very slow to recognise that Charles had not been a genuine ally. In fact it was only a couple of years later that we recognised that he was so power-hungry that he would have done anything to gain our alliance at that stage.

Simon Jansen, production director of a factory, was always yelling for increased worker productivity. His opponent, shop steward *Bent Olsen*, was always in a defensive position. They were enemies of long standing and didn't even respect one another. In fact, they mistrusted each other thoroughly.

Simon never succeeded in raising productivity, and, in consequence, Bent always negotiated from a weak position.

Neither Simon nor Bent had fun.

Uno Löfgren, managing director of a small furniture company, always brought the best out of his workers, although his opponent on the union side, *Kjell Ahlgren*, was a tough enemy to face.

Both Uno and Kjell had fun whilst fighting.

Analysis

Joan was a real friend, Harry a good ally.

Barry was also a good ally and indeed went on to be a good friend. We wasted a good deal of time with Charles and with David.

Simon Jansen and Bent Olsen never managed to raise

their vision. They found no areas of mutual interest in which to develop a win–win situation. Normally it was a lose–lose situation for both of them. Simon wanted higher productivity and lower costs, and Bent wanted higher wages and less work at the same time. They didn't even manage to find a win–lose combination, they just went on trying to beat one another.

Uno Löfgren and Kjell Ahlgren, on the other hand, managed to raise their vision. They found out that a change to more interesting and responsible methods for the work force would yield higher productivity and lower costs. Kjell's members had a better deal and Uno a better result out of the company. They also agreed that the fruits of higher profitability should be divided in a realistic way between the two parties. Both parties made more money for their stakeholders.

In time their alliance developed into friendship. They had fun.

The need for friendship grows more intense as managers move up the ladder. Increasingly their position becomes isolated and they are forced to consider and act on matters which they find it difficult to talk about with others.

The man at the top is particularly short of real friends. He finds himself isolated. If he is lucky, he may have a competent secretary who is privy to all his information and who is able to share and discuss matters with him, but the material to which he has access is often personal or so confidential that he cannot discuss it with anyone else inside the company. His wife (or her husband) usually lack the experience and insight which would enable them to do so. Such isolated individuals need to go outside for a discussion partner who can adopt the role of friend and confidant.

For the average manager not (yet) so isolated, friends in management are essential discussion partners.

Action Dos and Don'ts

DO
- Cultivate your friends. Take them into your confidence, be generous in your support, offer impulses, respect and confidence.
- Discuss the problems and opportunities surrounding you with friends.
- Build alliances. Be as open as possible, seek to understand needs, wants, hopes. Keep your integrity with allies.
- Find help to knock down the barriers of organisational enmities.
- Be frank with and respect positional enemies.
- Try to recognise the needs of personal enemies and work to reduce barriers; but do not be afraid to recognise that some clashes of personality are inevitable.
- Try to develop the attitude that there is always a win–win situation around the corner.

DON'T
- Presume that friendship needs no nurturing.
- Expect too much of casual allies.
- Ignore your enemies.

DO
- Find the best balance in your relations with those around you.

4 Company Culture

Part of the enjoyment of managing lies in the way we go about it; and that depends a little on ourselves, but much more on the organisation we work for.

Every organisation has its own character. It is rooted deep inside the organisation. It is very pervasive. It has a great influence on the style in which each manager operates within the organisation, and indeed on his behaviour outside the organisation.

If you are going to enjoy managing, the culture of your organisation is something you have to live with, and make the best of.

The culture of any organisation is easily felt, but not so easily described. At its deepest it rests on "values", which are known to everyone without their being consciously aware of it. Values comprise what is respectable in terms of quality, price performance, service level, respect for the boss, or what is morally acceptable.

Suppose, for example, that the person in the next office was found to be stealing stationery. You know perfectly well the reaction which would be created inside your company, but it might be a different reaction in the company across the road. You know, because it is part of the value-system of your company.

Then there are norms, myths and heroes.

Norms are the ways in which people behave. Since they are visible, they are more obvious than "values". There are norms about what is reasonable quality, about how hard we work and what is good behaviour and what is bad behaviour. Sometimes norms are conservative (as in a traditional firm or in a bureaucracy). Other norms can be very different: for example, in an advertising agency unorthodox behaviour and even unorthodox dress could be the "proper" way to show normal behaviour.

Myths – fables about the organisation's past achievements and failures – do the same job in the firm as fairy tales do for small children. They indoctrinate them with the "proper" models for behaviour.

Heroes are the embodiment of what is to be esteemed. Usually they are leading people, dead or alive, but they can also be the products of an organisation or even the spirit and style in which it is run.

These factors – values, norms, myths, heroes – characterise every organisation. They set it apart from the one next door. They are part of the very deep rooted culture of each company.

One aspect of culture is the way the enterprise is managed. This usually reflects some history and much of the character of the chief personality in the firm.

Some top bosses are very analytical. They use a pattern of managing which is rooted in pure logic. For them every situation has to be deeply analysed, and decisions taken according to the logic of the analysis – even the logic of the computer. Such decisions then have to be planned and implemented in some sound and systematic way – "doing it the intelligent way". Not for them intuition, "a feel for it", "seat-of-the-pants operation". It is a culture which influences the top man's close colleagues and spreads through them to be part of the way in which everybody manages.

A quite different culture is the one rooted in co-operation. In this culture proper behaviour is having people working together on decisions, projects, ideas, methods. The co-operative culture is based on winning the staff's co-operation.

Another way of managing is the competitive. This is a culture in which people are driven. They are kept constantly in a state of tension. They are expected to compete with one another, hard, for resources and for esteem.

Examples

Derek Short was a first-rate businessman, an imaginative, driving character. All the systems were set up to feed information to him: he took both key policy decisions and many day-to-day decisions which in other organisations might have been delegated.

Derek was surrounded by people who were heavily influenced by him and by his success. Their job was to implement the decisions which Derek took. They acted almost as additional limbs for him, enabling him to extend his spheres of operation.

Extend them he did, both in business and in private life. He even became a director of the local football club, where his personality enthused manager and team. Back at his firm, management and indeed the whole work force became infected by this enthusiasm and were to be seen going off together to matches both home and away.

Derek was an outstanding example of a charismatic personal leader and an entrepreneur, setting a competitive culture.

Ernest Brown was a very different character. He was a highly successful manager of a factory within a group of companies. The style within that group was co-operative, open, supportive. Whenever he found difficulties, a telephone call brought friends and allies surging forward to help.

Ernest was headhunted to work in another organisation. He became general manager of a factory which had been unprofitable. It was assumed from his excellent record that he would be able to transform this larger factory to profitability. Ernest found its systems were not working, that people had low commitment, that the factory had relied on craftsmanship which had declined to obsolescence through successive decades. Customers, equally traditional, were beginning to fall by the wayside.

Ernest's new chairman believed firmly in appointing people and leaving them to get on with running the job. He prided himself on appointing capable executives, and it was then up to them. Ernest strove manfully to set some priorities by which to tackle the muddle, but as soon as one problem was cleared up, another two or three were revealed. He worked intensely, at first inventively, but increasingly desperately, without any of the sort of support to which he had been accustomed in his previous factory. The subordinates whom he had inherited, expected him to solve all the problems. They had no experience of the supportive pattern of management to which he had been accustomed.

After eighteen months of struggling against the odds, never really enjoying it himself, and never to the satisfaction of his new chairman, Ernest went back to his previous employer. Brilliant manager in one culture; failure in another.

Ole Johansen was a bright and accomplished accountant. By good fortune, at the age of 27, he became one of the support group to a team negotiating massive international contracts, and his strengths enabled him quickly to become a full member of the negotiating team. He was competent, thrustful, ambitious.

In his early thirties, Ole was recruited to become finance director of another concern. This concern had been doing badly: its practices had become routine, the management was elderly, there had been little innovation either in products or in methods for very many years. The board recognised that new blood was needed and brought the youthful Ole in to take one of the key positions in the company – that of financial director.

It didn't work. Ole found that the methods all round him were decades out of date. He had no difficulty in perceiving how newer methods would help, but his colleagues and his subordinates were wedded to their traditional practices. They never quite understood, certainly never accepted, the force and the potential of the ideas which Ole was suggesting. He found himself isolated, with nobody to talk to, no friends, numerous enemies. He was totally frustrated by trying to introduce dramatic action into a routine organisation.

Roger Carlsson is a highly successful board member in a large Scandinavian bureaucracy. His power is founded in his knowledge of the company's technology. But nobody really knows him well. He is isolationist and analytical in his way of operating.

A brilliant strategist, he has manoeuvred his organisation through one crisis after another. He has produced results and (he says) he has fun. He is an example of an analytical manager.

Per Alm is another board member of the same company. He is what is best described as a "benevolent autocrat", loved by the more capable of his subordinates (whom he loves in his turn) and feared and respected by the less capable (whom he does not care too much about). Though not on the same strategic level as Roger Carlsson, he is producing at least the same, if not better, results from his part of the organisation. He is having fun. Strong people grow up under him: weak people don't.

Analysis

Each company has its own culture, deep rooted, which is set in a context – felt more than spoken – within which its people can manage.

Each organisation has its own culture, personified by the biggest boss and the way he goes about doing things.

Derek Short, Roger Carlsson and Per Alm are examples of people strongly personifying the following cultures of a company:

- Derek: The competitive driving figure.
- Roger: Analytical, logical, the strategist.
- Per: Do what has to be done through people, co-operation.

Ernest Brown and Ole Johansen are examples of managers, excellent in one situation, striving desperately and ineffectively when transferred to a different culture. Neither had any real chance of success in the new positions in which they found themselves.

How about your own situation? Are you and your organisation of very different characters? Try using the triangle below.

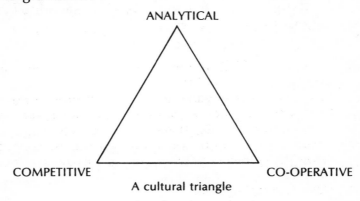

A cultural triangle

Put a cross either on one of the lines or somewhere inside the triangle to represent the sort of culture in your company: for example, a cross right at the top if it is a purely analytical culture; a cross right in the middle if it seems to you to be a blend of all three. Now put a dot to represent your own natural character and competence.

If your cross and your dot are far from one another, you are probably not enjoying your managing as you should be. You have the alternatives of changing your attitudes – and you will find that very difficult – or accepting that you are in the wrong firm.

Most of us work in less clear-cut situations. There is usually some difference between our natural character and the culture of the place where we work. But it is worrying, as are most situations we find hard to describe, and we yearn for change. What is to be done?

Stop worrying. You can only change the company's culture (1) if you are the top person in the organisation, (2) if you are deeply committed to the idea and prepared to take years at it, (3) if you have got very strong support and preferably the help of professionals in organisational change, (4) if you recognise that a number of people are going to be ruffled in the process and that you will need to surmount strong opposition. That's a tall order. Unless you are in the top position and have the power and the commitment, stop yearning for the impossible.

You cannot change it, but you might be able to change the way you adapt to it. Start operating more in line with the character of the company, and you will find that fitting into the culture can become enjoyable in itself.

To make the best of it, you need to:

● Recognise the distinctive way in which things are done in your own "firm".
● Learn to play the game according to those rules.
● Stop worrying about whether you can make the world a much better place to live in. You can't.
● Focus your ambition on what you can reasonably hope to achieve, playing the game by the local rules.
● Have fun doing that.

Action Dos and Don'ts

DO
- Accept that the culture of an organisation is very durable.
- Accept that one manager on his own cannot have much influence on it, unless he is exceptionally strong and at the top.
- Develop the way you manage to suit the culture of your organisation.

DON'T
- Seek for change in isolation from your colleagues.
- Hope to change style radically, quickly.
- Linger too long in an organisation demanding strengths different from your own.

DO
- Seek to settle in a firm with a culture which demands your own strengths.

5   Private Lives

It is a principle of this book that managing should be enjoyable: that a manager should so balance his interests and his role that he has fun while he is managing.

Managing in this fashion is very satisfying and very intriguing. It can become so demanding that it interferes with a manager's private life.

For a more balanced life, the manager needs to review the way in which he is using his energy. A simple device here is to consider time spent on work, family, other social activity (clubs, societies, pubs, etc.), and private time on hobbies and other individual interests. This can be shown on a cross, as in the first figure overleaf.

Notionally, a well rounded range of interests might give equal weight in all four dimensions as in the second figure. The workaholic, on the other hand, concentrates on the job, with a pattern as in the third figure. It's worth assessing for yourself the way your energy is being spent, and whether the balance is to your satisfaction or not.

Whatever the judgement, there is an overlap between your working life and your domestic life.

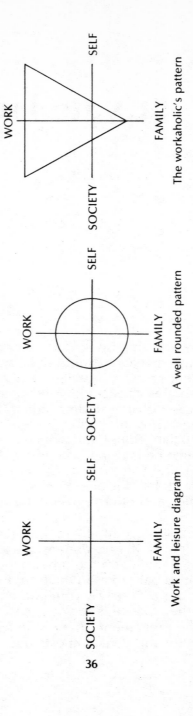

Work and leisure diagram

A well rounded pattern

The workaholic's pattern

36

Examples

Ian Briggs is departmental manager in a local factory. Day after day he takes his briefcase home late in the evening. He walks into the house, and, after perfunctory greetings, goes off to his study every evening and opens the briefcase. The study light is to be seen burning until 2 or 3 o'clock in the morning.

His wife provides him with supper about 9 o'clock and has to stay up to take his coffee at midnight. They have little social contact. His wife is ageing rapidly. He has little confidence in his staff and they all claim to be totally frustrated. His boss is highly perplexed about this. Whatever the boss says or does, he seems to have no influence, and Ian goes right on with his workaholic activity.

Our friend *John Goldman*, who quit one job when he found he was driving home more quickly than he was driving to work, was very different. Dedicated to his work, regularly putting in unpaid overtime, he switched wavelength totally whenever he was nearing home. A warm smile, an intimate greeting, interest in the family's affairs – they all seemed to come naturally. In addition he is heavily engaged in local activities.

Analysis

Those are examples of one life which was well rounded and of another which was heavily work-centred. How's yours? Use a cross such as the figure opposite to create a picture of the way your energy is going.

For many managers this is likely to be a picture heavily weighted towards work, with less emphasis on the family and social or personal activities than you judge to be ideal. If that is your situation, what can you do to improve the balance?

Surprisingly little. Things will probably change as your career develops (more on this in Chapter 17, Personal Goals). But right now you are attracted to work, you are committed to it, you enjoy it and you are anxious to go on enjoying and improving it. It is natural that it will continue to engross you.

You can, however, take some steps to prevent your family being undermined by your working habits, and to reduce the extent to which you become cut off from your family:

- Take one child out to dinner (or whatever they want) once every month. Just you and the child. Thus, if you have three children, you will have one evening alone with each of them four times a year.
- Book a weekend in the country for yourself and your wife or husband once every quarter. Give it overriding priority.
- Don't take work home. Work late at the office if you must; start early if you will. *Never* take it home.
- Control the work bubble. Too many managers at home have their thoughts focused on work. The family hubbub goes on around them, but they do not even hear it as they think about work. Consciously and deliberately as you are nearing home, switch wavelength. Start thinking deliberately about each member of the family and what he or she will have been doing, and about how to re-establish your relationships with them when you get home.
- Start positively. However tough your day has been or however worrying the situation, present to your family a mood which will help make them buoyant. If within the first minute you are home you can spread a mood of happiness and well-being, their night will be totally different from that created by the harassed gloom-merchant – which is what you were a couple of minutes before.

Action Dos and Don'ts

DO
- Periodically review the division of your energy between work and private life.
- Beware of the temptation of being caught inside a work bubble.
- Compose yourself and concentrate on the family when you go home.

DON'T
- Take work home.
- Expect total understanding and appreciation domestically of your work problem.
- Let work-gloom determine family mood.

DO
- Nurture your private life.

SUMMARY OF PART 1

This book is based on the belief that managers are busy people, whose greatest problem is to set priorities and achieve balances amongst many competing interests.

One essential ingredient is that they should enjoy the process of managing. They must give sufficient priority to creating the conditions for their own enjoyment. And even within that field of fun they must consistently balance a number of forces.

Each manager has his own reasons for being one, based on desires for achievement, affiliation or power. These desires spring in part from his own nature as it has been created in history. He cannot do much about that history – no more than any of his colleagues can do about their own histories. He can do more about the other aspect of his desire – his expectations. And theirs.

He needs to give his attention to his friends, his allies and his enemies. Sparkle with the first and nurture their friendship. Deal with his allies and find ways of working to mutual profit, and perhaps even convert some to friends. Distinguish between positional, organisational, and personal enemies, and find friends and advisers to help cope with them.

Each of us works in an enterprise with its own distinctive culture. For most managers it is not possible to change that organisational style in any substantial way. Each has to learn to adapt his own style to find out how the game is played locally, and to develop the skill of playing it that way. If he can't or won't develop that skill, he is not going to enjoy managing there.

An enjoyable business life absorbs a manager's energy often at the expense of his domestic and social life. He may need to give conscious attention to improving the balance between these different aspects of his life.

There are other influences on any manager's enjoying his job. He's not for long going to enjoy it unless he gets results; and he's not going to get results unless he achieves a position of adequate influence. These are the crucial fields to be tackled in the remaining parts of this book.

Part 2

RESULTS

THE ART OF MANAGING FOR RESULTS

INTRODUCTION TO PART 2

One field in which the manager needs to balance the forces at work is that of enjoying himself, having Fun. The next field is that of ensuring that he produces Results.

In order to do that he must adapt his role, reaching an executive position, and he must direct his efforts and strategies along sound lines. The skills of building the Ability to Achieve and of Directing form the subjects of Parts 3 and 4 of this book.

This part is concerned with the art of producing results. The forces which we must balance in this field are:

● Doing things himself.
● Seeing things are done by other people.
● Developing control systems.
● Thinking positively.

Each of these forces is the subject of a chapter in this part.

6 Doing Things

Most managers work both as technical specialists and as managers.

As specialists they use their expertise in the process or service which they are controlling. For example, the dyehouse manager with his expertise in dyeing; the chief accountant with his knowledge of accountancy.

As managers they are concerned with a different sort of expertise: that of planning, organising, leading and controlling. This is the expertise of ensuring things are done.

For any manager there is a need to keep a balance between

(a) doing things himself, and
(b) seeing things are done.

For most, the temptation is to do too much.

Succumbing to this temptation is natural enough. Most of us gain promotion in our careers because we have shown ourselves to be competent as specialists. If somebody wants a new sales manager, they don't start by looking at their least effective salesman. They probably start by looking at their most effective salesman: the one who knows how to sell; the one who knows he can do it; the one who is good at it.

Thrust into the new role of sales manager, this capable salesman has many uncertainties: he is inexperienced at the management component of his job, uncertain about it. He is uncertain about other people for whom he has responsibility, and about how far he can trust them. He is uncertain of the relations which he needs to form with a new group of managerial colleagues.

It is only natural that he should concentrate on what comes easily to him. He has a drive and a concern to succeed in his new role, and will automatically use his energy on doing the things which he knows he can do well.

For this ex-salesman, "doing things" takes the form of selling. It doesn't take the form of ensuring that things are done by other people, by the systems, and by the policy-makers.

In the next chapter we concentrate on how he should go about ensuring things are done, but, in this chapter, what he should be doing himself.

Doing things for the result-getter is a question of creating the milieu in which other people will do the production job, the selling, the accounting or whatever it may be. Such a manager takes time and effort to:

1. Create organisational charts for his people to do things.
2. Help them to think positively and creatively.
3. Create positive relations between his department and those of his colleagues.
4. Deal with blockages, of resources or in relationships, which obstruct the pathway to results.

His efforts focus on organisation, on negotiation, on delegation, coaching and counselling.

There will of course be occasions when he needs to use his outstanding technical competence. But, remember, when the sales manager is out selling, he is not managing. His success as a manager depends in part on the way he balances his managing role with his technical role.

Examples

Jim Baldwin was the epitome of a superb salesman promoted to sales manager. He was charming, knew his products, was respected by his customers, inventive, and a thruster for product development.

Jim was promoted to be sales manager in charge of ten area offices and a sales force of about seventy representatives. He worked intensely, put great effort into product development, and dealt personally with some thirty overseas agencies. He also retained strong contacts with many of his previous customers.

Unfortunately, Jim never found out how to delegate. He handled all the serious correspondence personally, chased the progress of major orders. He was so busy doing things that he did not worry about forecasting the market – he even disbelieved some gloomy predictions made by other people – and he never had time to go into it himself. At various times, promising members of other departments were assigned to help him, yet always they found themselves frustrated with little to do.

His charm and his imagination were such that he sustained the respect of those in authority for a very long time. He survived as sales manager for years, but they were years of increasing frustration for those around him, and of growing disillusionment as his colleagues found that sales were not coming in.

At the end of those years, no longer respected and admired, Jim left, firmly believing that all the problems derived from his colleagues.

Our old friend *Herbert Johnson* was totally different. He

is the chap who rose from cashier to managing director
(see Chapter 2).

During that career, whilst in his period as chief
accountant, he increasingly delegated all responsibility
for the production of regular control data. Having
surrounded himself by able and hungry young men, he
had no shortage of people ready and anxious to take on
those responsibilities. Freed from the day to day activity,
his concerns, interests, and whole pattern of thinking
became free to work on long-term issues, to build the
status and the influence of his job as manager.

Analysis

Managers must all have some technical competence, but
this is often at odds with their need to ensure things are
done through other people.

Jim Baldwin never discovered the art of delegation. It is
all too easy to continue to use technical competence and
to perform activities which could reasonably be delegated – to ignore the art of positioning, organising and
delegating which enables others to see things are done.
He didn't get the balance right.

Herbert Johnson had done his homework on delegation properly. He saw things were done.

At different levels in a company we have a different
proportion of the specialist component and the managing component in our jobs. The supervisor in a dyehouse
may spend 70 per cent of his time using his technical
expertise and only 30 per cent on his managerial
expertise. His boss's (dyehouse manager's) ratio might
be 50/50, whereas the production director should
possibly spend only 20 per cent of his time using his
technical expertise and 80 per cent his managerial
expertise.

Action Dos and Don'ts

DO
- Resist the temptation to over-indulge your technical skill.
- Do things which enable other people and systems to perform their duties.
- Take pride in ensuring that things are done.

DON'T
- Try to do everything yourself.
- Frustrate the aspirations of people in support.

DO
- Be lazy at times.

7 Getting Things Done

Any manager's job is to see things are done, and most of his success hinges on ensuring that people do them. The latter is so important that we're going to break it down into six component parts, and devote a section to each:

A. Knowing what should be done.
B. Delegating.
C. Organising.
D. Inspiring.
E. Acting as a catalyst.
F. Developing people.

A. KNOWING WHAT SHOULD BE DONE

To ensure things are done, one must first know what needs to be done.

It is a question of knowing what are the key areas

within which one's results have to be produced. That knowledge should be obvious from a reasonably composed job specification, evident from the normal pattern of communication between colleagues both formal and informal. The method of obtaining results should be flexible, with attention switching from area to area as circumstances and policies change.

It should be. Too often it isn't. There is a haze surrounding many managers, to the extent that they do not know what will prove to be reasonable results.

Here is one method that has recently been introduced to help managers to clarify their duties. It is the use of some simple ideas called "The Trim Philosophy" (or "getting into good Trim").

The stages of this process are:

1. Define your key result areas. Choose the three or four such areas in which you believe it is most important for you to achieve your aims.

    One such area is usually customer services, using the term "customer" to cover customers elsewhere in one's company just as much as customers outside it.

    Examples of other areas include market development, departmental costs, recruitment methods, quality assurance, staff development.
2. Define output in each area. Ideally put figures to the output. If you find that impossible, write down in words some description of the output.
3. Compare your output with that of your "competitors". Any imbalance?
4. Define alternative levels of output from your department. If the figures (or words) previously defined represented 100 per cent, what would represent 80 per cent? What would represent 60 per cent, and what 120 per cent?
5. Ask your "customers" inside or outside your department, how they would react to the different levels in terms of willingness to pay the price.

Examples

Anders Hansson produces results. He is the head of a maintenance department in a pulp mill and is responsible for some 400 men.

He worked through a Trim programme for his department. His first step was to look at the objectives and long-term goals of the division and from them to derive objectives for his department.

He defined levels of service which he could offer in terms of planned maintenance, long-term and short-term, and of emergency services. He then set about discussing with his customers (the other departments) the alternative levels of service he could offer, and their cost.

It was not treated as a paper exercise, figures to be inserted into a computer. It was used as a tool for discussion between colleagues, so that he could find out the results that he was expected to produce, and so that his colleagues would know what they could reasonably expect.

Anders went on to plan how to achieve that level of service which his customers required, to organise and to develop his staff and systems accordingly.

Anders achieved four sorts of result:

- Departmental costs down 20 per cent.
- Improved service.
- Understanding colleagues.
- For himself, more certainty, more job satisfaction.

Comment

This is one example of the use of Trim philosophy to help managers to know what needs to be done.

The important issue is not that you have to use the Trim philosophy. What is important is that you need to know what you have to accomplish. Ideally, know it in terms which are understood by and acceptable to your boss and your colleagues.

Informal discussion or semi-formal meetings help you far better than a mass of paperwork and computerisation.

However you go about it, knowing what needs to be done is the first step towards seeing that it is done.

B. DELEGATING

In getting things done through people, every manager has to strike a balance. Two extremes between which he has to find his point of balance are delegating too much and delegating too little.

Some managers lazily stand back and leave people to do things in their own way, without really managing at all.

However, in our experience the majority have the opposite problem: they cling too tightly to responsibility themselves, without delegating. It is understandable, since often they have been promoted from specialist to becoming specialist manager. It is the old problem of the sales manager better at selling than at managing.

Each of us must find a balance. Here are a few ideas which we have found helpful in deciding how to delegate.

First, the concept of Time Span of Discretion. Each of us does a job in which he is supervised from time to time. For the salesman whose job is to visit customers that supervision might come on the occasion of his weekly meeting with his branch manager. If the branch manager then checks how many calls the salesman has made, how many orders he has taken, what other results he has achieved, he is checking that salesman weekly. The salesman's time span of discretion is one week.

The branch manager, on the other hand, is probably not checked by his boss so often. He might, for example, be checked on the branch's progress on the occasion of a monthly meeting with the regional manager. This branch manager then has a time span of discretion of one month.

For the regional manager reporting to the sales manager, the corresponding time span might be quarterly. And so on up the chain of command.

Another helpful device in delegating is the "Why, What, How" hierarchy. Let us describe it.
Think about your job.

● *What* do you do?
● *Why* do you do those things? Indeed, *why* does the job exist?
● And *how* do you do your job?

Given that you can distinguish the difference, you can arrange the queries in a hierarchy:

● *Why* you do things.
● *What* you do.
● *How* you do it.

The *Why* is a matter which is certainly of concern to our bosses. The *What* may be – it depends how much they delegate to us.
But if we have a really competent boss, one who has ensured that we are adequately trained and shaped for our job, one who will be accessible if there is a rare emergency, then we do not want him interfering with *How* we do our job.
Competent delegators leave the *How* to their subordinates and encourage them to take maximum responsibility for the *What*.

Examples

Michael Kane was in charge of a design team which included six draughtsmen. One of them, old Bob, had been working in the department for years. Michael well knew that he could trust Bob a great deal and left him on his own for anything up to four months to carry on with the design of a specialist order.
Young Bruce was recently qualified, and obviously

couldn't be trusted in the same way as Bob. Michael made a point of checking his work weekly, but also made a point of trying to extend that time span. Bruce performed well. His time span of discretion was up to two weeks within the first couple of months; and by the time he had been working for Michael for six months, Bruce had a time span of one month.

Three examples of departmental "managers" from the academic world, Kenneth, Leslie and Martin. All were professors.

Kenneth prided himself on having recruited a strong staff during his tenure of office. He was interested in their research and in their writings, and took the trouble to find out about their progress regularly, offering what constructive suggestions he could. He worked on the *Why* and the *What*.

Leslie, equally proud of his staff, was very much more deeply involved. He wanted copies of any papers written, he criticised and changed parts of them and insisted that his name appeared as a co-author. He took a much greater part in the *How* than Kenneth.

Martin was a great ideas man. Whenever he found himself with a member of his staff, the ideas poured forth. His staff member would then go off enthused and develop a plan to put the latest idea into practice. Meanwhile Martin would fly off to give a seminar half way across the world.

Coming back, finding the staff member at the airport, Martin would burst out with the new range of ideas which had occurred to him in the 'plane coming home. He never had the time or the interest to consider last time's idea and how far his people had gone in developing it.

Analysis

Michael Kane, the designer, made deliberate use of time

span of discretion. He used it in his discussion with his people, so that they knew how he was trying to give them a chance to perform. He used it as a tool in deliberately developing his staff and delegating to them more and more as their abilities developed.

Each of us has discretion to conduct his activities as he sees fit within some time span. We need supervision, guidance, counsel, at some such intervals – or we are called upon to take more responsibility than we are paid for. On the other hand, if we are subject to checks too often, we are oppressed. Between these extremes is some time span in which we can exercise our discretion to our own satisfaction and to that of the people above and around us.

In their various academic departments, Kenneth was greatly respected. So was Leslie, but his staff hated working for him and resented his lack of delegation.

Martin, constantly enunciating fluffy ideas and never following them up, enthused successive staff members, who tried their best to make something of his brilliance. Too many of them fell by the wayside trying, and Martin's brilliance was never reflected in the eminence of the positions he achieved. He was a poor delegator because he would never follow up.

C. ORGANISING

Are you happy about the way things are organised in your department? Many managers of our acquaintance are not. They feel frustrated and inhibited by the organisation.

As far as the formal sense of the organisation structure is concerned – the sort of pattern which is defined on an organisation chart – there is not much they can do about it. That organisation chart can usually be changed only in the context of some mammoth reorganisation, outside the scope of any particular manager. It is, moreover, such a time-consuming process, and the end-product so troublesome to implement, that most structures last a long time. People have to make the best of them.

How then do we suggest making the best of your organisation? The greatest possibilities lie in informal discussion with all around you, helping to ensure mutual understanding of what needs to be done, and how people need to work together.

The starting point is the range of Key Result Areas already discussed in Section 7A. When you have defined your dozen areas, you need to check them systematically with your boss. You need to make sure your subordinates, your colleagues and your customers know what you are trying to achieve, and receive their reactions to your Key Result Areas. You might even ask your subordinates and the men next door which of your key result areas they think is the Critical Result Area, i.e. the one that you must attend to now.

The next step is the drafting of a job specification. Jobs change slowly but inexorably in any dynamic organisation and it is worth trying annually to write down your present duties and responsibilities. Keep it rough. Use it as a basis for discussion with the boss, with colleagues, with subordinates. Make sure that it covers both the key result areas and those other areas which are routine yet necessary for you. All the items in the job specification should be defined in terms of result or output. If you can't describe an output, that item is just an activity, and who wants to pay for an activity that doesn't produce anything? Use the job specification drafting and discussions as a means to agree with your colleagues items where you need jointly to work with them and to take joint decisions.

Next step: develop a "supplier" list. Just as we show in later chapters the need to recognise who are your customers, so also you have your suppliers: people whose support you must have if you are to perform your job effectively. People who can wittingly or unwittingly impede your producing results. List them. Seek out and ensure that they are conscious of your dependence on them. Convert them into friends and allies.

Having defined all your personal key result areas and having encouraged the people around you to do the same, next step make an integrated list of the various key result areas. Together the areas define the "business mission" of the department in question, and constitute a form of job specification for a whole department. You can be confident of the effectiveness of your part of the organisation if such a job specification is genuinely approved by neighbouring departments – both "suppliers" and "customers". Take the opportunity of such an annual routine to bring those departments into your affairs; and be glad if they are sufficiently interested as to suggest some minor modifications – for example, transferring some of the result areas between adjacent departments. Think positively and negotiate constructively with them.

There will be times during your career when you feel that the organisation is more seriously impeding your department. It will probably be impossible to introduce a radically new organisation structure; yet you may feel that more is needed than the annual discussion of individual and departmental job specifications.

When you feel that the time is ripe for such extra action, start by asking each of your "suppliers" and your "customers" to define their views of your department's key result areas and critical result area. Bring them together and ask them to make presentations of their expectations of your department, as evidenced by those areas. Lastly, show them what were your own expectations of your department. Ultimately, reshape your own expectations and ensure that you, your suppliers and your customers emerge with compatible expectations.

If in doubt about the reframing of a particular expectation, bear in mind that the crucial question should be "How can we serve the interests of our 'customers' better?"

Such processes of discussing result areas and job specifications are likely to take two or three days of your time. The benefit will be twofold. There will be a shift in the formal organisation – departmental and personal jobs will be modified. More significantly, the organisation will be more effective: there will be a reinvigorated basis for communication and co-operation, and united expectations of what should be achieved.

Such an expenditure of two or three days will pay handsome returns if you make it an annual event.

D. INSPIRING

The ability to inspire rests on some qualities we cannot easily influence, and on others where we have more hope of developing our talents.

One aspect is charisma: that subtle aura which surrounds any human being and which enables some to sparkle as inspiring leaders. Charisma is innate. It's deeply implanted in us. History has made it for us, and we cannot easily change it.

More important for most of us are the qualities which we can develop. Qualities such as cheerfulness, positive thinking, warmth of personality.

People respond to openness. The greater the extent to which you are frank in telling people about the pressures you are under – the personal relations (with colleagues, etc.) which cause you difficulty, the market and other pressures around you – the greater the extent of their responsiveness, concern and, usually, confidence in you.

People respond to vision and far-sightedness. A good subordinate whose time span of discretion is three months will be looking forward beyond that. He will be thinking of his work within the context of six or nine months ahead.

If you have a subordinate with a time span of three months, your own is probably six or nine, and you will be looking forward beyond that to two or three years ahead. An insight into that longer term seems visionary to the subordinate.

Generosity is inspiring. Generosity not in terms of

money, but in terms of the sharing of ideas, of acclaim or achievement.

It is not only such benevolent activities that inspire subordinates and colleagues. People respond also to a little anxiety. The creation of a little tension. The administration of a merited rebuke.

Examples

Derek Short, you may recall, was the leader blessed with tremendous charisma. His personality bubbled over, his drive engulfed the many people near him and, through them, spread to influence hundreds of people.

As a rule such leaders keep very close to the work that is being done. They do not delegate readily. Their subordinates work on a short time span of discretion. But the power of the personality, the strength of the charisma, is such that they are inspired to perform.

At the other extreme, *George Reid* was far-sighted, high in achievement and affiliation but low on power. He set his subordinates to think far into the future and to control their efforts at that lengthy time span.

His frankness, openness and vision inspired subordinates. They were led to see visionary possibilities of what they might do in their jobs and to perform with whole-hearted commitment. Things were done.

He was also generous. Travelling by train one day with a pile of paperwork to catch up with, he found that one of his companions was a trainee who was conducting a project within his company. They were soon engrossed in discussion of the project, and George – as was his wont – turned the conversation towards career development. The trainee was a girl called *Kathy Hall*, and as a consequence of the discussion she started to take a qualification in works management. It was at that time a rare qualification for a female.

George's paperwork didn't get done on the train; but Kathy went on to get her qualification.

Herbert Johnson, the power-oriented cashier who grew to be managing director, was equally open and frank in his dealings with subordinates. He was constantly discussing with his bright young staff the things he was trying to do and the problems he was coming up against. They were able often to recognise for themselves the contributions they might be able to make in the common interest. He was an inspiration.

Herbert was also good at inspiring colleagues who were friends or allies. Through his visionary qualities and his generosity to them and to their interests, he won their accord and their support. But he was less open in his dealings with those whom he saw as enemies to be manipulated if there was to be much hope of progress.

The following anecdote cannot be camouflaged, and we are indebted to the principal figure for permission to make use of it. Our friend Leif tells the story.

He arrived at Stockholm International Airport with the president of S.A.S., *Janne Carlzon*, who is renowned throughout Scandinavia for having dramatically boosted the Airline's performance.

They landed late one night from abroad and, in company with other travellers, they waited for their baggage. Each passenger of course carried his full allowance of Duty Free – it is a treasured boon in a country where alcohol costs about three times as much as in Britain.

Suddenly – crash – some poor traveller had dropped his bottles and they had shattered.

"Instinctively", says Leif, "Janne Carlzon stepped forward and gave his bottle to the poor unfortunate. I was astonished and asked why he did it when it was not even S.A.S. responsibility. Baggage is handled by the airport authorities not the airline. Janne's reply when I asked him was that the passenger is unaware of who runs the baggage facility and he, the president, is determined that his customers will gain a positive impression of S.A.S."

The prompt gift of that bottle of whisky immediately became known throughout the baggage hall. Within minutes, word of it had spread through all S.A.S. staff at the airport and the incident was common knowledge throughout the airline system within twenty-four hours.

Astonishing maybe that one bottle of whisky so generously and instinctively presented could promote so much customer and employee goodwill.

The majority of us do not have such outstanding personalities; but we do have the ability to increase our openness and our vision.

The instinctive gift of a bottle of whisky startled all who saw it. Corresponding generosity at work, with ideas and with support, is another way of inspiring people.

E. ACTING AS A CATALYST

In chemistry a catalyst is a chemical which, without itself changing, causes a change in the relation between other substances.

In managing an enterprise, a catalyst is a manager who sparks off new ideas or new relations among his colleagues. He is one who helps them to set off on new ways of working.

The manager who wants to act as a catalyst has a number of devices he can make use of:

● *The committee structure of his organisation.* The places at which we can dangle far-sighted visions, invite colleagues to suggest creative possibilities, spark off new ideas and activities.
● *Project groups.* Bringing together people from different departments and different interest groups

to work together on a satisfying project, order, idea, etc.

● *Ideas engineering.* Bringing his own work-people together, possibly with representatives from other groups, and encouraging them to produce their own ideas about how to deal with a problem.

● *Management-by-objectives.* In its purest form, management-by-objectives is a process in which the manager discusses with colleagues and subsequently with subordinates why actions are needed and what needs to be achieved. Keep it simple, and this process can be extremely productive and helpful to the process of seeing things are done. Complicate it – draw up a battery of papers and forms and rules – and this means of management degenerates into a bureaucratic ritual. Keep it simple!

Examples

Herbert Johnson was a great user of committees. He ensured he was on important committees himself, saw that his cadre of friends and allies were on more committees, started up a number of extra committees. He used them both to promote his own ideas, and to act as a catalyst for his colleagues. Some of the phrases he used in the latter role were:

● "Is there anything that could be done about . . . . ?"
● "What is the problem facing us in . . . . ?"
● "What results do we need to achieve . . . . ?"
● "What would be the best way of . . . . ?"

Stein Rham was technically incompetent in his own trade as head of the department for internal education in a middle size Scandinavian firm. He was, however, always extremely positive and cheerful. He greeted us: "Hello

Bill, hello Sven, how extremely nice to see you again –
what shall we do this time?" He really never understood a
thing, and to accomplish anything in that company we
had to by-pass Stein and talk to other people.
Nevertheless, he made people happy and cheerful, he
acted as a catalyst, and his department was seen to
produce results.

When UK Government declared that a particular year was
to be "Quality and Reliability Year", most companies
apparently did not even hear.

   George Reid did. He set out to use the theme in his
company. As part of her personal development, he gave
Kathy Hall the task of running a twelve-month project
encompassing everybody throughout the company – it
then had 2,000 employees in half a dozen factories.
George himself acted as chairman of meetings of senior
management to launch the initiative, and Kathy was very
active in travelling from factory to factory, bringing
groups of managers and work-people together; broad-
casting bright ideas around the group both by news-
sheets and by word of mouth; giving prominence to
success stories.

   As the gospel spread, so Kathy used ideas engineering.
She did little herself but, acting as a catalyst, made the
group highly quality conscious and quality efficient. It
was also very good for group morale and for Kathy's
self-development.

Two of our client organisations tried to use management-
by-objectives. In the company of which *Gordon Dennis*
was managing director, it was treated very simply. People
wrote down key result areas and their targets, by hand
and on plain sheets of paper; but discussed avidly with
bosses and with colleagues. Three months later the
dog-eared bit of paper would be brought out again,

progress checked, lessons learned both from success and from lack of success, and the next quarter's plans/ targets prepared. It worked, and for several years was a key tool in the running of Gordon's company.

In *Wallace's* company it was set up with much more of a flourish. Elegantly printed forms, special files for each manager, copies distributed and filed. Somehow this exercise never produced any physical effect other than the mountain of paper.

Analysis

An effective manager acts as a catalyst. He uses committee structures and project groups, ideas engineering and any other device he can find to help his colleagues and his supporters to keep things moving.

F. DEVELOPING PEOPLE

The best form of management development is a good boss.

There is no substitute. A good boss will expect much of you, help you remove impediments, and leave you to get on with it. A poor boss will cramp you and expect you to clear the impediments on your own. When you come up against the awkward people in the next department, he will say that it is all the fault of your personality – but he is only partly right on that.

Apart from his continuous inspiration and support, the good boss also uses a number of tools to help people develop their competence. He uses:

- Coaching.
- Counselling.
- The discussion partner role.
- Job reviews.
- Project work.

Coaching

The art of coaching is to make staff conscious about the way they are handling situations *as they occur,* then and there, on the job. Not only making them conscious of such experiences but also learning from them.

The good boss is constantly hunting for events he can use for coaching. Important events of a sort which can be recognised at the outset and which can be discussed again after they have been dealt with.

At the outset the coach's questions are:

- "Have you thought of various ways of tackling this?"
- "And of the alternative consequences?"

After the event, fundamental questions are:

- "What did you learn from this?"
- "What are you satisfied about? What would you do the same again?"
- "What would you have done differently?"
- "Which one of your assumptions turned out to be wrong?"

Counselling

A rare opportunity when boss gives subordinate a chance to state what he thinks is going well in the job and what not so well; and when the subordinate can get the boss's view in a reasonably long term sense. Once a year.

Discussion partner

The best discussion partner is one with whom one can sit down and be made to think. The really good discussion partner helps one to clarify one's problems, to think through what could be done about them, to see fresh possibilities, to settle on a course of action, and to accept that some difficulties just have to go on being accepted!

This is the sort of thinking which is meaningful when one does it for oneself. It is not meaningful when one's partner supplies all the answers.

A good discussion partner helps one's own thinking rather than imposing his own. He is a good listener.

Job reviews

A good developer uses the redrafting of job specifications as a development tool. He uses it as a basis for discussion of responsibility and authority, and of the partnership between boss and subordinate. Contrast the boss who regards redrafting a job specification as a paper exercise.

Project work

Giving responsibility to an individual or to a special group, to tackle some particular problem or opportunity. Full-time or part-time, possibly over a period of several months.

Examples

Erik Jonssen was mentor to one co-author *Sven Söderberg* during Sven's early years in consultancy practice. One day he asked Sven to go with him to a board meeting of a client company, when there was to be a discussion of a proposed investment in a new project. An innovator in the company had been working on the idea for several years, developing technology way ahead of the main stream. Should the company invest more heavily in this high-risk project?

Sven thought that Erik had asked him to join the meeting because of Sven's interest in the subject of creativity, but later Sven realised that Erik was at least equally concerned to make use of this as a coaching opportunity.

Driving to the client's office, Erik talked at great length about the personalities on the board:

- Knut, managing director, ex-marketing, an open and honest chap.
- Henrik, finance director, living in the world of figures.
- Jon, a divisional director; very forceful personality.
- Lars, an elderly stubborn man who headed another division; very sensitive to personal criticism.
- Karl, brilliant research director.
- And there was Ralf, the genius behind the concept; shy and retiring, and expecting that justice would reign, that the merchandise would speak for itself.

Sven was bored by Erik's description of the people, which went on and on throughout the journey. Erik asked him what he thought they would decide and Sven answered reluctantly that obviously the board of such a company must be competent.

When the board came to the interesting item on the agenda, Ralf made a rather bleak figure. Not a salesman exactly. No elegant presentation. He assumed that everybody on the board knew all about his development and its brilliant possibilities. He did very little to project the idea.

Henrik (finance) immediately asked why it had already cost so much without producing anything, and why Ralf never seemed to keep to his scheduled times. Ralf replied meekly that development did not work like a railway and that unforeseen snags constantly had to be dealt with.

Henrik smiled and said that if he tried to run the finance department on that basis, the company would be dead in no time. Karl (R & D) made a long speech critical of Ralf. And so the discussion went on until eventually the board turned down the proposal.

This story does not end there. Five years later, Ralf was given a prestigious public award for his concept, which had been published in the technical press. The board belatedly allotted funds to Ralf and at last he was showing a profit for the company.

Driving back, Erik asked Sven what he had learned from the board meeting. Sven thought about it and came out with such answers as:

- "Well the first thing that strikes me is that board members are fairly normal people."
- "They do not work with brilliant logic."
- "They work according to the same laws of politics and ill-founded intuition as most of us."

Erik asked Sven what he would have done differently if he had been in Ralf's shoes. Sven thought that the most significant thing he could have done was to make an ally of Karl (R & D) at an earlier stage. Karl's thinking by now was not positive: it was in fact very negative, influenced probably by seeing an invention competitive to his own department.

Sven did not think Ralf learned much from the episode, nobody coached him, but Erik coached Sven often and very regularly. Sven will always be grateful.

The other author of this book, *Bill Scott,* had a brilliant boss. Regularly, about every six months, Bill would go to the boss for a counselling session. For about five minutes he happily let Bill tell him how he was getting on and the problems he was up against, but very quickly the boss would turn the session round. He had Bill counselling him, commenting on and sometimes even criticising the things which Bill saw him doing, especially with other colleagues. It was good for both of them.

Simon left university at the same time as a class of thirty other engineers. He went off to work in Namibia and found himself under a managing director who believed in challenging his young men. Before long Simon was out in the backwoods, remote from any boss, running a small local contract. He grew in experience.

Soon the managing director had him running a bigger site. So it went on.

A couple of years later, Simon went home on leave and attended a celebration party with a dozen of his erstwhile university contemporaries. They had been working in very restricted jobs, and there was an enormous contrast between the mature and successful manager and those who had been restricted. Simon was quickly bored: "They were like a lot of school kids." He left the party quite early on.

Analysis

Erik Jonssen made positive use of coaching and greatly helped his people's career development. Within consultancy, of course, there are abundant opportunities for such coaching. But opportunities also abound in other sorts of enterprise. Every customer complaint provides an opportunity for coaching. Every need for a new method. Every organisational problem. Every innovation. There are so many coaching opportunities that one can only take advantage of a limited number. Have you got the balance right?

Kathy Hall's work on the quality and reliability project is one example of the way in which an individual can be challenged to produce high results and can develop in the process.

Counselling and reverse counselling help both parties.

Simon's growth on the job is good evidence for the belief that "the best form of management development is a good boss".

SUMMARY OF CHAPTER 7

Ensuring that things are done through people depends first on knowing the areas in which it is important to be effective, and knowing what performance level will best serve the company. The Trim philosophy is one way of going about it.

Delegating properly is a matter of setting the right balance between delegating too little and delegating too much. Useful aids are the Time Span of Discretion and the "Why, What, How" hierarchy. Good organisation also helps.

Inspiring other people – subordinates and colleagues – depends in part on aspects of our personalities which we cannot easily change. It depends also on our openness, our vision and our generosity.

The catalyst triggers off actions by other people. Committees provide a setting, and alternative tools are project groups, Ideas Engineering and informal Management-by-Objectives.

The developer's tools are coaching and counselling, discussion partner and job review, project work and project groups.

But never mind about the tools, the fact is that some bosses try hard to challenge and to lead other people towards accomplishment. The tools are less important than the attitude.

Action Dos and Don'ts

DO
- Clear your thinking about what has to be done.
- Make use of your subordinates. Help them to be ambitious and help them to find their way round or

through blockages.
- Help your organisation to help people work together.
- Be open and generous in your treatment of your friends and allies.
- Try to act as a catalyst.
- Help your people to develop their talents.

DON'T
- Do what others could do for you.
- Assume that what needs doing is obvious.
- Over-restrict your subordinates.

DO
- See that things are done.

8 Control Systems

Control systems are tools which should enable managers to check that things are being done.

An ideal control system would be one which enabled a manager to be given timely information. To know that progress was in line with intentions. To know what aspects of his job could be left alone, secure in the knowledge that they were running satisfactorily. To recognise where other aspects were deviating so that attention could be focused on them and corrections made.

Such an ideal control system would provide a yardstick by which to tally his success. It would be a helpful and benevolent tool.

That would be in an ideal world, but real life is often far from the ideal.

Examples

Axel Green and *Saul Blake* were two eminent industrial-
ists. Each headed a massive group of companies with
many subsidiaries. They had different titles (in one case
president, in the other case chairman) and they were in
different countries, but their control systems had a great
deal in common.

The way they made use of those control systems was
radically different.

Axel believes in Management-by-Objectives. He has a
one-page list of key results for each of the subsidiaries,
relating to plans put forward by the subsidiaries and
approved by himself. In his executive office he has a
computer display where he can order up any of the
subsidiary "pages" (up-dated monthly). He uses these
displays as bases for telephone discussion with each
managing director. The MDs of some of the subsidiaries
were interviewed by the authors, who found that they
liked the system very much. They appreciated the contact
with the president, they found his thinking ever positive,
they were able to share their concerns with him and to
receive help in solving their problems.

Saul Blake had a similar system in that he had a range of
figures up-dated monthly for each of his subsidiary
companies, and used those figures as bases for telephone calls. There were, however, two major differences. One was that the figures were of conventional
accounting ratios, not key result areas. The other was
that the MDs lived in terror of the monthly telephone
calls. There were so many ratios and so often the
accounting process masked a few details, that it was all
too easy to pick on suspicious figures. Days of important
time were spent trying to anticipate where Saul's eye
would light, researching why particular figures looked
poor, checking through the accounting detail.

Derek Short was a charismatic leader whose personality

and energy radiated and enthused all around him. Derek's way of controlling was simple. As managing director of an enterprise employing 700 people, he had control information fed to him weekly. He expected key figures to be with him by Monday of the week following, and fuller analyses by Wednesday. Everybody was invited in, upbraided where appropriate, told what to do, enthused by his personality and sent off to get on with it. "Everybody" extended to some forty people, and as Derek was a busy man, it was a question of three or four minutes apiece.

Sounds awful! Not the sort of thing any consultant or author could admire: but then there were plenty of consultants who went in year after year, suggesting some new system. Their advice was often adopted, only to drop quickly into disrepute. Derek controlled in the way that Derek controlled. His people responded to that method. His personality enthused them. Things were done. The company extended, its wealth increased. Crisis lurked close, but nothing would influence the nature of the company's life-force – Derek.

George Reid's control was utterly different. George was the chap who surrounded himself with "hungry" people, a lot of them hungry young people. He raised their vision, led them to set themselves challenging objectives, was ever ready to talk with them but frankly expected – if they were the sort of people that he wanted – that they would look after the results themselves.

Failures received short shrift but, given the extent of the autonomy which he left to his people, the infrequency of his control, it was astonishing that the failures were so very few and so very far between.

Herbert Johnson used committees as the cornerstone of his control system. One of the first examples was when he brought together the cashiers from other branches to discuss how they might together cope with a new piece of government legislation. It was a useful meeting, discussion ranged over quite a lot of interesting points as well as the legislation, and the cashiers agreed to meet from time to time. The cashiers' liaison meetings became established as three times a year events at which Herbert acted as convenor and chairman, and one of his bright young men acted as secretary. They wrote minutes and distributed them widely in the company.

Herbert also had a daily morning meeting in his own office. His main people gathered with him for twenty minutes or so to open the mail, check copies of yesterday's outgoing correspondence, feed one another information, discuss the day's activities.

Herbert also set up a reporting system, widely circulating within the company information which built up in his department.

A couple of years later, by which time he had become chief accountant, the "cashiers' liaison meeting" had become a key part of the company's financial control. One of Herbert's bright young men was convening the cashiers' meeting, and Herbert had established two other systems.

The first was the quarterly finance control committee. This was established because the board of directors were all full-time executives and extremely busy men. Set up "to help them", the finance control committee consisted of the three most prominent directors with the chief accountant (Herbert) as secretary.

His own department's affairs Herbert managed through a monthly progress meeting. He took a full two days to review everything that was going on inside his department.

These were the key control systems which Herbert used.

Noel Blackburn was a bustling managing director, full of

novel ideas. He was a glutton for control, constantly demanding new sets of figures and new routines, keeping his finance director for ever extended on the production of more and more data. Frankly the systems did not always work perfectly. Each new system had its own teething troubles, but meanwhile the evidence of the new system suggested that something was seriously out of control. Noel's dynamic energy came to grips with the problem. He zoomed in, made changes, but somehow control eluded him.

At yet another extreme were our clients in local government. No names now. It was the system which dominated. There was a wealth of controls, a wealth of controllers, a wealth of concern that the controls should show the right results. Managers became the captives of the system. Their concern was to show the right answers in the control system. These nominal results were seen as much more important than the real effectiveness of the local government operation.

Analysis

These are examples of different control systems and of different ways of making use of them. Axel Green's use of key result areas and of positive thinking was found to be positively helpful by his people. Saul Blake's use of conventional accounting ratios and of threatening telephone calls had the opposite effect. Now, ten years after the time when we first observed these systems, Axel's group continues its purposeful progress. In Saul's company many MDs left and the group decayed.

Derek Short, George Reid and Herbert Johnson each control in ways appropriate to their temperament. Derek with his typical sense of urgency and immediacy, George with long-range vision and goal-setting, Herbert through his skilful use of committees.

Noel was obsessed by systems. He made such intense use of them – including untried systems – that he over-controlled.

Of course, in the bureaucratic world the system can really take control, stifling people and results.

Action Dos and Don'ts

DO
- Use systems to feed you information on what is being done.
- Check on results more than on methods.
- Use your control system in conjunction with positive thinking.
- Give mature subordinates maximum freedom.

DON'T
- Control too much.
- Control too often.
- Control too deeply.

DO
- Keep it simple.

9 Positive Thinking

Who do you go to when you want to test out your bright ideas? To check and improve the ideas before you put them in front of other people?

You almost certainly go first to a positive thinker. One whose automatic reaction will be to look for the positive possibilities. Through him, you will achieve three things: you'll build your confidence; you'll see even more scope for your ideas; and you'll find the negative aspects put into perspective.

How many people approach you in the same sort of way, looking for positive help? If the answer is fewer than you would like, then this chapter is for you. In it we shall briefly explore four types of thinking:

● Negative thinking.
● Vague thinking.
● Selfish thinking.
● Positive thinking.

We all know about *negative* thinking. We have met it in

some such comments as the following:

- "It won't work. . . ."
- "If you had been working in this operation as long as I have, you would know what it is possible to achieve. . . ."
- "There is no room in the budget. . . ."
- "Let us put it on ice for a while. . . ."
- "We've always managed very well without. . . ."

This is negative thinking.

Negative thinkers have a defensive attitude. They see any new situation as threatening and something they need to be very wary of.

If you hear a person say "Yes, but . . ." you have met a negative thinker.

One expert in the field of such thinking talks about "Automatic NO-response". He says it goes back to childhood. He argues that when the toddler experiments with pulling tablecloths, toppling flower vases or un-plugging electric plugs, parents automatically say "No, No". This, he argues, conditions the infant to be scared of new behaviour, an insecurity which has devastating effects on the person's later adult thinking.

A particular type of negative thinking is *critical* thinking. This type focuses on looking for weaknesses and is highly developed in academic circles. Indeed, ability to "dispute" was at one time lauded in degree ceremonies. Such critical thinking, however, is not central to the role of profit-making organisations. It may be helpful to have a critical thinker acting as a Devil's Advocate in the later stages of projecting a new idea, but earlier he'd strangle it.

With *vague* thinking, a topic is seen as significant and as having dozens of different aspects to it. The topic remains vague unless thinking is sharpened, unless the mass of material is analysed into a sufficiently small number of sections to become actionable.

Vague thinking is not a sign of immaturity. Rather it is a sign of intellectual laziness. Our brains cannot normally handle more than a few ideas at the same time. One psychologist talks about "the magical number Seven plus or minus 2". He states that we can only take in chunks of information that are of this magnitude. But one of the authors of this book says firmly that this is more than he can cope with. Unless he can organise his thinking under four headlines (plus or minus 1), his brain is over-whelmed.

Selfish thinking is the sort which can only contemplate something from one's own point of view. Other people's ideas are either completely dismissed or totally re-arranged into one's own shape.

And finally, there is *positive* thinking. Positive thinking always sees new opportunities in every situation. If you hear someone say "Yes, and . . .", you are facing a positive thinker. You will find that he:

● Explores new and interesting aspects of what you have just been saying.
● Helps you to take your own idea a stage further.
● Looks for something useful, even in apparently stupid ideas.
● Learns from past mistakes.
● Talks more about the future than the past.

Examples

Herbert Johnson, the up-and-coming accountant, at one stage found difficulty in making progress because some branch accountants were dyed-in-the-wool traditional-ists. His positive reaction was to bring them into his central organisation and give them senior posts of some consequence in which they could use their strengths to advise branches on routine matters. Meanwhile, the branch accountant positions were filled by some of Herbert's own bright young people.

Impending mergers create some of the most traumatic situations for managers. In the period during which the merger is threatened and in the aftermath of inevitable reorganisation there is overwhelming uncertainty.

Anxieties grow. In part they grow for real reasons: the manager used to operating on a time scale of two or three years recognises that reorganisation will shift the situation so radically that it has become pointless for him to take far-sighted actions.

This sort of real problem is compounded because of the unknown. He sees a host of forces which are vague and overwhelming.

Arthur Brown was in just this position. An excellent and far-sighted manager, active and energetic, he found that a merger was threatening. His role would almost certainly disappear if the merger were to take place, and whilst his strengths were such that anybody else could see that he should positively benefit in status, Arthur's anxieties grew to the point at which he started taking tranquillisers.

One of his colleagues, similarly placed, was fortunate to have the advice of a consultant who helped him to sharpen his thinking and to overcome this type of problem. (See advice below, p. 86.)

Bo Jacobson is the managing director of a division within a Swedish group of companies, his operations having a turnover of some £200 million. He turned those operations from a substantial loss to a 20 per cent return on assets in less than one year. As we spoke to him one night, he said: "I am still working 20 hours a day and I love it, but this is not challenge enough for me. I want something really tough to get my teeth into."

Lennart Nilsson, a Swedish consultancy friend of the authors, was not re-engaged by a client-company after having been their consultant for some fifteen years. His immediate reaction was: "This is very good. It is a good thing for them (the new management team) to earn their wings on their own. And it is a good thing for me to be forced to replace this client with something fresh and challenging." As far as we could judge, this came from his heart.

Three of us were waiting to drive off on the first tee at the golf club. Alf asked me: "How are things with you?" "Great", I said, "I've just become a grandfather." Alf said: "The day my grandchild was born, I remember. . . ."

It was a story which went on until we had putted out on the second green, and by then Alf's companions were thoroughly bored by the topic of grandchildren.

A couple of weeks later, Alf asked why I had never told him I had become a grandfather. He was such a selfish thinker that he hadn't taken in what he had heard on the first tee.

Critical thinking has been a hallmark of academic competence. One university department which we know well, authoritative and highly respected in the academic world, holds weekly staff seminars. Eminent visitors give papers at those seminars. Invariably, whatever the merits of the speaker, new ideas are criticised, new analyses are pulled to pieces. Attention always focuses on deficiencies, never on the creative possibilities.

Analysis

The distinction between positive thinking and negative thinking is one of attitude. The attractions of positive thinking were positively outlined by Dale Carnegie with sufficient force to influence the attitudes of a generation of Americans.

To overcome vagueness of thinking, analyse. Make copious use of paper.

Think in a sequence of stages:

● *A mind-clearing stage.* Jot at random on a sheet of paper every aspect of concern. Having cleared the mind, discard the paper.

● *Analysis stage.* To analyse, use any three or four headings which you can think of which will enable you to sectionalise the problem. If you have difficulty in identifying three or four suitable headings, try one or two of the following classifications:

   (a) Satisfaction and disappointments.
   (b) Threats and opportunities.
   (c) Costs and consequences.
   (d) Problem-solving approaches (see Chapter 14).
   (e) Any three headings plus a "dustbin" for items which don't fit.

● Decide action.

What if you find that at the end of this exercise there is no action you can take? Arthur Brown was in fact in this state as the takeover loomed over him. The consultant who helped his colleague made a simple suggestion. "All right, then, set down the earliest date at which there will be a possibility for you to take action."

The date was about six months ahead. It was astonishing to find how the mere act of setting down this date took the worry out of the situation through that six months.

How do you help a negative thinker on the road towards becoming a positive thinker? It is extremely difficult because the "No, No" attitude is so ingrained in our characters. But once we appreciate the difference between negative and positive thinking, there are three steps we can take:

1. Be aware of our own negative thinking. Take note of how much we use the phrase "No, No", or "Yes but . . .". Once we become conscious of the habit, we can start to compensate.

2. Adopt the following slogan when anybody puts a new idea to you: "That is fine and let me add at least one extra reason why this idea is realistic."

3. It can sometimes be helpful to go through the following exercise:

- Describe at least one vision for the next couple of years.
- What will the world look like in terms of your vision eighteen months or two years from now?
- What is the first step that will take you in that direction?
- Which person/s will you use for support?

This chapter has been designed to encourage positive thinking. It is intended certainly as strong counsel to overcome vague thinking and selfish thinking.

There must be some balance between one's use of positive thinking and one's use of negative thinking. Not every idea will ultimately prove to be practical.

The message which we hope shines from the chapter is that it is all too easy for us to strike a balance in too negative a fashion. All too easily we can strangle creative possibilities.

You will probably find your Results improve if you shift the balance towards more positive thinking.

Action Dos and Don'ts

DO
- Look for creative possibilities.
- Eliminate vagueness.
- Consider events as opportunities.
- Test yourself *now*. Develop one positive vision.

DON'T
- Concentrate on the difficulties.
- Go on worrying.
- Tear every idea to shreds.

DO
- Strike a positive balance in your thinking.

SUMMARY OF PART 2

This book is based on the assumption that managers are busy people who have to set priorities and maintain balances.

One major field which has to be balanced with others is that of producing results; and within that field each manager must consistently balance a number of forces.

He must be active, doing things. The things he does as a manager should create conditions in which others do things on his behalf. When the sales manager is selling, he is not managing.

Managing is seeing that things are done. In consequence, the manager must know what should be done. In doing his job, he delegates, organises and inspires, acts as a catalyst, and develops people.

He has to give enough attention to control of progress. He has to strike a balance between too much and too little control, too often and too seldom, between results and methods.

He has to maintain a balance between positive and negative thinking.

He has to balance the attention which he gives to each one of the forces. Together they can help him master the art of producing results.

Part 3

ABILITY TO ACHIEVE

TAKING UP POSITION

INTRODUCTION TO PART 3

The ability to achieve influence is the theme of Part 3. It is one of the four key FRAD fields which have to be kept in balance – making it enjoyable (Fun), producing Results, Achieving the Ability to influence events, and heading in a sensible Direction.

To achieve influence a manager has to:

- Have a chance to perform.
- Develop a sense of timing.
- Relate to colleagues and staff.
- Improve his position.
- Organise himself.
- Develop his personal skills.
- Adapt to his "customers".

This part of the book devotes a chapter to each of these seven aspects of the Ability to Achieve a position of influence.

10 The Chance to Perform

Any manager who is going to see things are done must reach a position in which he has the possibility of acting.

There is no point in striving desperately if shackled by surrounding circumstances. You need:

- a supportive culture,
- a patron,
- competent subordinates,
- internal marketing.

The need for a supportive culture was discussed in Chapter 4. If you are the sort of person who wants a secure environment and a steady job, you are not going to have much chance to perform the way you want to in a company that is constantly innovating. If, on the other hand, you thrive in conditions which challenge your creativity and which make heavy demands on your energy and commitment, you won't find much chance to perform in a world where routine reigns.

A precious asset for any manager is a good boss: one

who can challenge, delegate and support. But what of the manager who feels himself saddled with a hopeless boss? Many people feel so saddled. Some of them really are and can do little about it; but for most there is some positive action which can be taken.

Whoever the boss, it helps to have some other patron who will give you his backing from an authoritative position.

Action through people also means good subordinates. You need a strong team.

In addition, you need internal marketing, to promote your interests to your colleagues, to be discussed in Chapter 12.

Examples

Owen White was the sort of man who took an adequate degree at university, but spent far more time whilst he was there in organising undergraduate societies. The Archery Club, for example, grew from a membership of 32 to 97 whilst he was its secretary.

On leaving university he joined a state-controlled transport organisation, and discovered by bitter experience that he was not very good at dealing with the routines of bureaucracy. After two years trying, he changed jobs and found himself working in George Reid's company.

Dramatic challenge. Ambitious projects. Demands on his imagination. Highly supportive colleagues. High expectations from all of them about what he ought to achieve. Owen thrived.

Paul Wood had a similar background in university and early job experience. He moved on to work in Noel Blackburn's company. Paul's great problem was that he was too far down the line from Noel to be able to do much on his own initiative. He was blocked by a boss who was a superb thinker but never achieved any innovation.

Paul recognised that the progress control system in his department had broken down, but his immediate boss blocked all efforts to introduce a new system. Paul persevered. He waited until the boss went on holiday, then, in three hectic weeks, sold his suggestions for a new system to Noel Blackburn, sold it to the managers of the neighbouring departments, sold it to the supervisors and operatives in his own department.

That took one week. The second week was a hectic period of installing the new scheme. The third week was an even more hectic period of dealing with teething troubles.

By the time the boss got back from his three-week holiday, Paul had the system installed.

Bengt Larson was a capable young market analyst working in a medium sized Swedish company. He was on bad terms with his boss, Hans, the marketing director. Their work overlapped, there was a personality clash, and their relationship became very poor.

Bengt took outside advice and decided to leave the organisation. He moved to another group of companies where he did a splendid job and his reputation grew in Swedish professional circles.

He was recruited back to his old company, where Hans had now climbed to become managing director. Bengt's role was that of chief executive of a new subsidiary. He was now no longer reporting so closely to Hans and they were able to build a fresh respect for one another's abilities. Hans now speaks very highly of Bengt.

Ralf was one of our examples in Section 7F. He was the brilliant inventor who went to an important meeting and put up a pathetic performance. His excellent ideas were squashed and he didn't then get into a position to perform.

Herbert Johnson was a master at internal marketing. He constantly met influential people, discussed ideas with them, ever careful to help them recognise those aspects of his intentions which would be of benefit to them. Ever minimising the disadvantages. Ever far-sightedly suggesting possibilities to mutual advantage. Constantly using the committee system to improve his chance to perform.

Analysis

If your surroundings of culture and boss unite to shackle you, there is not very much you can do. Owen White and Paul Wood are both examples of high performance people who were frustrated by their surroundings. Both of them moved to companies with, for them, higher potential.

Owen was lucky enough to stumble into one in which the challenge and the possibility to perform were dramatically high. Paul, on the other hand, had to find ways of evading a confining boss; and he was fortunately able to win the help of Noel Blackburn as patron for his project.

Bengt Larson's case illustrates positive steps to overcome an apparently bad boss. Bengt acted as follows:

- Analysed the problems he was getting.
- Recognised that some were his fault.
- Proved his ability in another setting.
- Managed (in the end) to develop a positive relationship between himself and the boss.

The consequences included improvements both in his own performance and in the boss's.

Ralf was dreadful at internal marketing. He failed to do

his homework properly, he did not set out informally to influence his colleagues, he did not seek to gain their interest. His presentation of his ideas was pathetic. He badly needed training in personal skills (see Chapter 15) and he could have done with a strong patron.

Herbert Johnson has now become a well known figure in this book. He surrounded himself with people of high quality. He had their backing and their commitment. They contributed heavily to his success, his ability to perform.

So did his internal marketing.

If you feel that you are constrained by your boss, do a little testing. Think through the causes, some of which are doubtless his fault. Some, but not all: there are others which spring from you and your way of operating; and still others which come from the way you and he manage your relationship.

See if you can find some topic on which you and he can work together – some proposal or some problem which needs to be solved. When you have finished it, try to start a discussion on the way you have been working together in that episode and take it from there!

Excellent bosses attract excellent subordinates. You need to recruit excellent people, to inspire and develop them, and you also need to lose the mediocre. Those of us with loyalty to our subordinates tend to be over-protective of them. We try beyond reason to sustain the weaker members, to develop them, to compensate for their under-performance and to use their colleagues to help compensate. We are, of course, right to do so for some time, but we are weak if we let that time persist too long.

Give him a year. Do your best and get what help you can. If he is still under-performing, you must let him go.

If you have to lose him, be sure that he has been set challenging targets in a previous period; then try to sit down with him, make an analysis of his strengths (oh yes, he does have strengths – not the ones you need, but others) and discuss with him where those strengths might best find a suitable outlet.

Action Dos and Don'ts

DO
- Work on your relationship with your boss.
- Seek visibility and high level influence.
- Acquire strong subordinates.
- Market your position internally.

DON'T
- Expect to be given total freedom to perform.
- Hide your light under a bushel.
- Try to do what you are not good at.

DO
- Work for the chance to perform.

11 Timing

A sense of timing is one characteristic of an effective manager.

One particularly sensitive time is the moment of taking up a new appointment. The impressions which other people form of a person during first brief contacts stay with them for years afterwards. They affect his later ability to perform.

It is difficult at that early stage to behave "correctly". The newcomer, probably brimming with hope and expectation, does not know the types of behaviour which are esteemed. Maybe it is wise to be quiet and respectful until one has absorbed a little of the culture? Or is he expected to be dynamic and outgoing?

Scandinavian managers seem to be more conscious than their British counterparts of the art of timing. They use the word "ripe" in a way which is not found in Britain.

They talk of a situation being "not yet ripe". They recognise that for any idea there is a ripening time, and they become adept at plucking when the time is ripe.

People also ripen. They may not be ripe for some activity or some responsibility today or this year, yet they may come to be ripe tomorrow or next year. People may even recognise that they were ripe for something yesterday or last year, even though no opportunity arose for them.

Examples

In the early stages of my working in a new job, my boss took me to attend a meeting with eminent people. I thought that I ought to make my presence felt and contributed two or three times to the discussion. Both then and now, I feel that these were sensible and intelligent comments, but the episode created serious problems which it took me years to live down. For one thing, I had sat in a chair which was normally used by some important person. For another, the way in which I made my "reasonable" comments was not appreciated. Both actions were seen as unwarrantably provocative.

The chairman of that company was an extremely powerful and remote character. I barely shook hands with him during my time in the company. In a subsequent appointment elsewhere, and by now much better attuned to the need to build a good contact network, I was in the healthy position of being able, within two or three weeks of starting, to establish contact with the chairman and quickly to win his esteem and support.

Then I was quietly warned off by my new boss, and a few weeks later the chairman was unseated. I'd started off on the wrong foot again!

Tore Kant was the head of a very large bureaucracy. His board members were in their late fifties and early sixties – polite, nice to each other, listening to each other's reports at board meetings. It was all very calm and frankly just a bit boring.

Tore had numerous friends in business. Often he gained from them the feeling that their board meetings were quite different. He was nevertheless surprised by what he saw when he was invited to advise in a board meeting at a friend's company. There was lively discussion and debate, and a wealth of positive thinking, with the board working as a team and its members building ideas and opportunities together. There was even a sense of excitement. It didn't seem anything like as calm as Tore's board meetings. What is more, when he spent the afternoon being shown around the company, Tore found the same spirit reflected throughout the management.

Tore went home with a new vision. He sensed that he would like to see his bureaucracy changed towards the sort of open, loyal culture he had just seen.

Being old and wise, he took time to reflect on the situation. He wasn't sure quite how he should tackle it, but he did know that the moment was not ripe for such a change and that it would take a long time before people ripened.

A few days later, he simply mentioned during a board meeting: "I am inclined to hire a coach to help the team." Nothing more was said. The idea of the "coach" cropped up at opportune moments during the next few months, his colleagues becoming attuned to the idea and even beginning to look forward to it. Eventually, after about nine months a consultant was introduced to the board at a two-hour meeting, purely on a get-to-know-one-another basis.

One outcome of that meeting was the thought that possibly the board members would consider teamwork further. That idea also had to ripen and it was another four months before the next step.

The board then went away to a conference centre for two and a half days. During that time they worked up their own views about the criteria on which to judge whether a team is effective.

This had a dramatic influence. Suddenly the board was ripe to develop a new way of going about its affairs.

Tore shared their enthusiasm; he and his board members now shared the same vision.

Gordon Dennis directed a number of clothing factories. He held a management development meeting with his fellow directors every three months. At one meeting, Victor Murray (Production Director) talked about his concern over the management of one factory. The manager in charge, Walter Donaldson, had been in post for fifteen years and the time was ripe and over-ripe for some change. The problem was that Walter was an excellent servant and there was no larger factory to which he could be promoted, nor even an equivalent factory to which he could be transferred.

Later in the meeting, there was discussion of the load on the directors. It was agreed that the Managing Director, Gordon, was over-burdened. It was not the first time that this problem had been raised, but now there was growing agreement that Gordon was tackling too much detail in contacts with the two main customers.

They were vital customers, between them accounting for 60 per cent of sales volume: they insisted on dealing direct with the managing director and they were of course insistent on detail. Gordon was finding that 80 per cent of his time was taken up on selling, with the inevitable consequence that the managing director was not spending enough time managing.

A new idea gradually emerged. Why not create a new role of sales director? Gordon could then handle only the top level contacts with the key customers, maybe once every two or three months, and all more detailed discussion with them could be handled by the sales director.

As that job was discussed and the beginnings of a job specification forged for it, Victor asked the key questions: "What are the strengths we should be looking for in this job?" Further discussion led people to recognise that it would be a very difficult job to fill. The strengths needed were a knowledge of the merchandise, attention to detail, an ability to interpret customer needs to design staff, and plenty of perseverance.

Once that was established a gleam appeared in Victor's eye, but, waiting for the moment to ripen, he kept very quiet. His colleagues became increasingly concerned that it would be impossible to recruit anybody with these qualifications. Waiting until they were really worried, Victor timed the question absolutely rightly: "Well, shouldn't we look to see if there is anybody inside the company with those qualities?" Victor was ever careful to avoid suggesting any name – he waited until the suggestion came from his colleagues.

Walter Donaldson was very satisfied with his new role of sales director and made a great success of it until his retirement ten years later.

Anders Hansson is head of the maintenance department in a pulp mill and he is responsible for nearly 400 employees. We met him in Section 7A when he used the Trim method.

When he first took up his appointment, he was appalled by the slackness of time discipline in the department. People didn't arrive on time at the start of their shifts, nor were they too fussy about the time at which they left. His immediate thought was that he would have to start imposing strong discipline, but that is almost impossible in the context of Swedish laws about democracy at work. Anders went to see Leif, the consultant friend who appeared in Section 7D. "How do I get people to accept their working hours?", he asked.

Leif suggested that imposing discipline was the wrong approach to the problem. He and Anders then designed a project. In it, Anders and his managers and the shop stewards together worked through an analysis of what people demanded in their working situation in order to feel motivated. They analysed the demands which the company made on people working for them as well as the demands of the people.

Together they developed an action plan aiming to make Maintenance a winning team. They had previously been looked down on by other departments, but now the aim was to be seen as leaders.

It could not be done in a day. There had to be a lengthy period of development and training of supervisors and of middle management, numerous discussions with the workforce, very heavy demands on Anders's disposable time.

The result has been a dramatic change in the use of time. Timekeeping is no longer a problem and there is a marked increase in the pride of belonging to Maintenance.

Bob Moore, 42, was divisional director of a mechanical engineering company. He had fifteen years' managerial experience and had been in his present job for four years. He was well in control and was beginning to find it boring.

His division made fruitful use of consultants, mainly from one well reputed firm with whom he established good relations. He was impressed by the consultants personally and by what he learned about their life. He gained the impression that they were constantly dealing with interesting situations, digging their teeth into fresh problems, and never having to put up with stupid subordinates and colleagues as surrounded Bob himself.

Bob had a chance to join the consultancy, and gladly said "Yes". He liked his new job and quickly found that he was working on an assignment making heavier demands on him than he had ever encountered before. He was at first nonplussed – it was just so different from what he anticipated. But after a while Bob began to cope. Thereafter things worked out quite well for him, and his clients began to talk appreciatively of him. He found himself working very hard and then, somewhat reluctantly, he agreed to act as manager to one of the consultancy divisions.

He worked harder than ever, but again, a couple of months later, he was depressed. "I just can't understand how other people manage it – they all meet their budgets and they don't seem to be working very hard at all!" But three months later Bob was again coping with his new job, meeting his budget. Asked about the difference, Bob said simply, "Well it seems I've got adjusted now".

Analysis

The examples started with two instances of moving into a new company and not being able to conform to the company's conventions. Lasting damage to the possibility of later being in a position to achieve results was quickly and accidentally committed. The newcomer was unwittingly rocking the boat. He would have done better both times if he had made less of an impact at the beginning.

A sense of timing was vital for Tore Kant. He sowed seeds with his colleagues and let them grow for nine months before making any significant move. Even then it was only a tiny move, and he allowed plenty of ripening time.

His vision has not, of course, been achieved overnight. It will take many years before a new method and a new spirit permeates his great organisation, but Tore's sense of timing enabled him to surmount the first critical hurdle of winning board enthusiasm.

A sense of timing is important in the long-term sense of waiting for events and people to ripen. It is important equally in the short-term sense, such as choosing the right moment to say something in a meeting. Victor Murray realised that Walter Donaldson might make a sales director but that was a revolutionary thought for his company. Traditionally production and sales had been different sides of the coin. Nobody had ever imagined that people might be interchangeable between departments. If Victor had spoken too quickly, the idea would have been laughed out. He waited for the right moment, asked the right question, with results satisfying to everybody.

Anders' great worry on timing was that of timekeeping. He succeeded in developing a winning team, proud and time-conscious.

Bob Moore's experiences were typical of those one meets with in any job. Assuming one stays in it for several years, one's mood and activities will pass through four phases.

First, assuming that the manager is moving voluntarily towards a new job that he wants, there is a *joining* phase in which there is excitement. He looks forward to new opportunities, new challenges, he meets new people and acquires new interests. At the same time he begins to absorb a new culture which has its own restrictions.

Within a couple of months, he is into the second phase, that of *adjusting* to the new situation. Still fresh with ideas and with possibilities, he now has a growing sense of the restrictions. He may even have doubts about his own adequacy – "Maybe I will not manage to cope with this job after all? Maybe my incompetence, up to now known only to myself, will be revealed to important people?" Gradually he accepts reality for what it is. In essence he is saying to himself, "Well here I am, this is how it is, let's make the best of it". He begins to learn how to play the game according to the local rules.

The third phase is *exploiting*. As the partnership of employer and employee develops, it is important for him to understand the realities of esteem in the enterprise. He needs to find out what is esteemed, what sort of dress is approved, what sort of behaviour is acceptable, what sort of internal politics exist, whose esteem matters, what friendships should be cultivated, whose friendship is the kiss of death.

Then comes the process of ensuring that he interprets signals from his surroundings. That he forms sufficient contacts to know what is going on next door and what is going on at the far end of the company. He needs to develop sensitivity.

The fourth phase is one of *diverging*. He becomes disenchanted with the situation, people around become disenchanted with him, or maybe he just grows old and runs out of vigour. Satisfaction and achievement both decline and at the same time performance and contribution are seen to be declining. No longer is he at one with the job: they are diverging.

Once that phase of diverging gets under way, it is almost impossible to get the paths (the job and the person) converging again. Disenchantment between individual and company grows – often rapidly.

Sometimes the individual clings tenaciously to a job long after the diverging has become apparent. This is harassing and stressful for him and for his colleagues. Far better for him to take the plunge and to leave at an earlier stage.

Bob Moore went through those phases. We first heard of him as a successful divisional manager but he was becoming bored, diverging from the job satisfaction he had had. As he moved to his new job, he first of all felt satisfaction, then became depressed before adjusting and learning to do the job. He exploited that job for about three years and ultimately accepted promotion.

Once again, after starting enthusiastically he became depressed and had to adjust rather painfully to the new role. He has been doing well in it for about three years but, knowing Bob, we suspect that he will soon be diverging. We think it won't be long before he is actively looking for something new.

Action Dos and Don'ts

DO
- Be cautious when taking up a new appointment.
- Recognise that your early enthusiasm will necessarily be followed by a period of adjusting.
- Let situations ripen.

● Recognise that people, yourself included, are constantly ripening.

DON'T
● Rush your fences.
● Let opportunities wither.

DO
● Develop the art of timing.

12 Colleagues

In Chapter 3 we discussed friends, allies and enemies in the context of enjoying management.

Colleagues affect our enjoyment, and they also influence our ability to achieve a position in which we can take effective action.

The man next door is always likely to cause problems. It is a fact of life. When he is the manager in the department next door, we have still, somehow or other, to cope with the facts of life.

The problem is that small incidents mount up, then begin to grow into suspicions and doubts about our neighbour. Unwittingly we find ourselves taking positive initiatives to prevent him causing us trouble.

He sees us as the man next door. Molehills quickly grow into mountains and relations all too easily deteriorate. The departments become competitive more than co-operative.

The remedies are of four main types.

Exploration. Take the trouble to sit down with the man

111

next door and discuss points of overlapping interest. Talk about your respective responsibilities, your objectives, your needs for support, your growth opportunities – the things that you could do together to make life better both for one another and for the enterprise.

Problem solving. There are bound to be problems. Do not just sit back and fume while the problems worsen and the relationship decays. Collaborate.

Using diversity. His interests are different from yours. There are bound to be some where your objectives diverge from his. Recognise, discuss, and agree on how to cope with those differences – do not waste energy fighting over them.

There are other points where his interests are not competitive with your own. Moreover, he has strengths which you do not have and vice versa. Make the most of your complementary interests and strengths.

Communication. Make a point of regular contact. Check what is going on in your respective patches.

Examples

Noel Blackburn's factory operated in three main departments, working a 168-hour week. The departments were preparation, production and maintenance.

The three departments hated each other. Supervisors in the departments were plainly unco-operative with one another.

It is well known in the industry that some materials can cause production difficulties even though they are within normal quality control limits. A quiet word from the preparation supervisor to the production supervisor could help the latter prevent production difficulties, but preparation supervisors and production supervisors were not on speaking terms.

When the maintenance department wanted to carry out a periodic inspection of a press, somehow it was always at a time when production priorities were overwhelmingly important. When a new electric lead was needed for a bit of borrowed equipment, the electrician just could not be made available.

Noel knew this was the situation but could not find the right key to open it up, until recession hit the company. They had to close for a couple of days and Noel took the opportunity to bring all the supervisors together with a consultant.

They spent the first day learning to know one another, discussing topics which were relevant but not highly contentious – a few general exercises on things like positive thinking.

By day two they were ripe for some joint problem solving. They spent the morning in small groups: the members from one department worked together, setting down areas where the interests of the company required that they have the co-operation of the other departments. They talked of responsibilities and objectives. Then they regrouped, each supervisor with a colleague from each of the other departments, to discuss the same issues.

During the afternoon, each supervisor was asked to identify his own toughest problem in relation to the other departments.

Each then sat down with two other people, one from each department. Each trio was challenged to find the solutions to the problems. After an hour, rather to their surprise, fourteen of the twenty supervisors discovered that they had the means to solve the long-standing impediment.

So, of course, they were told to go and sort out the other six problems. The consequence was a solution to nineteen of the twenty long-standing difficulties. The twentieth? "What it comes down to is that there is nothing we will ever be able to do about it as long as Mr Booth is the production director. But at least now we all know that, and we recognise that we have to live with it."

The result of the meetings was in one sense the solution of problems. In a different sense it was the creation of a new and positive team spirit within Noel's company.

This new co-operation was effective for several months but began to fade thereafter. It was the sort of co-operation which has to be boosted from time to time with smaller versions of the same problem-solving meetings.

John Ericsson is plant manager of a cardboard mill. He has six main departments – material supplies, production, warehousing, delivery, maintenance and quality control.

The plant was in a turmoil. One symptom was serious problems with wastage, which was ruining results and drawing the wrath of the board. It was even threatening to insert a new plant boss over John's head.

The members of the team at the plant were at one another's throats. Some of them refused to speak to each other. Something had to be done.

John talked to his consultant and, on his advice, took the management group away from the site to discuss their problems. The consultant asked them what they saw as their key problem, and before long received the answer: "We need to find our way back on speaking terms with one another."

The context was the high wastage rate, and the consultant asked how the cardboard was made. As is often the case in similar long-standing technologies, he received answers in terms of manipulating the equipment, sometimes successfully and sometimes not; but no real answer to the question of how the cardboard was made. The crew were surprised to find it so difficult to explain the process. Soon they were talking together and building a "theory" of their own. They were beginning to work together. The consultant peppered the development of their "theory" with very short lectures on the way groups of people work together, pointing out how they were developing. Gradually they became more open and constructive with one another.

During a couple of day-long meetings, the group

managed to produce a theory of what happened during the manufacturing process. They produced a list of factors which contributed to the abnormal wastage, and then put the list in priority order. Task-forces were assigned to each of the top three problems, and efforts made to identify the causes of each problem. The respective members of the team felt that they could contribute to all the questions with their piece of the jigsaw.

One result of this exercise was a decrease in wastage of 8 per cent, which was a very good result. Possibly more important, the psychological gain was the creation of a unified and purposeful team.

Analysis

Relations between adjacent managers can all too readily deteriorate. Departments become unco-operative and even hostile unless positive steps are taken to sustain their co-operation.

The example from Noel Blackburn's company, the warring supervisors, can be seen repeated in all sorts of organisations and at all sorts of levels. In principle, it is exactly the same as the sorts of relationship amongst the top executives of massive international groups. The interests of the marketing director, the comptroller, and the company secretary can breed conflict of just the same type.

Prevention is better than cure. Prevention by exploration and discussion of overlaps of responsibility, objectives, growth opportunities.

Both Noel Blackburn's supervisors and John Ericsson's management team used down-to-earth problem solving as a means to rebuild their team spirit. They then found they were drawing on one another's diverse abilities.

And they recognised that communication is a necessary vehicle in moving from hostility to co-operation.

When faced with a situation like one of those

described, go next door and say: "We have a mutual problem and I am keen to see how we could tackle it together." Wait. Give the other man an opportunity to exercise some leadership in moving towards tackling the problem.

Ideally, use the "golf club" or "walk-in-the-wood" tactic. Get away from your normal environment where you are steeped in day-to-day problems and problematical relationships, to an environment of open and friendly relationships: the golf club, the pub across the street or (if you are Finnish) the sauna.

Use diversity. Recognise that the man next door, say, could probably help you improve your day-to-day planning, but is not as good as you are in dealing with the union representatives.

Action Dos and Don'ts

DO
- Explore your overlapping interests with colleagues.
- Collaborate in solving problems.
- Use your different strengths to support one another.
- Make a point of regular contact.

DON'T
- Believe that he is deliberately stupid, offensive, arrogant, hostile.
- Let sores fester.
- Try to do it all yourself.

DO
- Work positively with colleagues.

13 Improving One's Position

Too many managers wander around complaining about their impotence. They talk about their lack of authority and about the problems created for them by some other amorphous "them". Often they think that they need to fight against their colleagues in order to win more power.

For some, fighting is fun; but for most, fighting is counter-productive. There are better ways of improving one's position.

First, try negotiating rather than fighting. Define what it is that you want. Is it more responsibility? What responsibility? Or more authority? Or is it the need to join together more actively with other people in making decisions of mutual implication?

Who else would be affected if you got your way? How can you help them? Negotiate.

Not all power and influence has to be won at somebody else's expense. There are plenty of ways of increasing one's own. Here are some examples.

Examples

John Goldman's ability took him from a respected position in a division to the corresponding position at group headquarters. His new role gave him the possibility of influence throughout the country, where he had previously been restricted to a particular county.

John seized the opportunity. He was soon known and regularly seen journeying throughout the group. Hundreds of people came to recognise and respect this estimable figure. He built enormous influence throughout the country whilst colleagues, nominally of more authority, stayed at base issuing edicts that were never respected.

Herbert Johnson, the cashier who went on to become managing director, was an expert at building power and influence. He was, of course, expert in accounting matters and devised plenty of systems. Indeed he regularly presented papers at international symposia and acquired a powerful aura. He built his position through seeing that he was on the right committees and on the right distribution lists, and gradually – as befits the emergent figure in a traditional organisation – he began to claim respect for his expertise.

He was generous. He did favours. He received favours in return.

Jim Baldwin, on the other hand, was unassertive. At meetings he would sit quietly, rarely saying a word. When the chairman asked him for comment, he was hesitant and indecisive. A superb salesman in the outside world, he was remarkably reserved as a manager within his company. Far too reserved to have adequate influence even on his sales force.

Fred Baker built his influence both by activities inside his organisation and outside. On the right committees. On the right distribution lists. Office in the top corridor. Secretary of the company's golf society, arranging the company's matches and playing with the right people at least once a month.

Rune Edgren is vice-president and industrial relations director of a very large organisation. Since childhood he has been trying successfully to gain influence and power. He never really hurt anyone on his way. He is seldom outside his office, and rarely seen outside company headquarters, but he has established an intricate web of formal and informal communication networks which keep him well informed. People talk of him as the expert on how the organisation really works.

Rune does favours for a chosen number of people. He is not greatly respected, mainly because of his lack of generosity to people lower in the organisation. He is considered to be very formal.

Analysis

Ralf, the brilliant designer who did not sell his ideas (Section 7F), did not get his position improved. He did not even perform at the level demanded of his position.

On the other hand, most of the examples above are of people in various ways improving their positions. They are ways which fall into a general pattern.

One way is by settling into a position near the centre of influence and power in one's own department, company or group. This is a combination of physical positioning (an office or desk in the right place), of role development (sitting on the right committees, for example) and of moving close to the central people. There is a jargon-word to describe this sort of influence: it is *centrality*.

Then there is the "out and about" quality: the extent to which a manager is seen to be out and about and influencing. The sales manager wanting influence with his production colleagues, and in the production lines where the goods are actually made, will not have much influence if he has never been in the factory. John Goodman travelled throughout his group, massively enhancing his influence.

There are other forces you can use to increase your influence.

Information. Be on the right distribution lists. Find out what is going on both through the formal system, such as the distribution lists, and through your own informal communication network.

Knowledge gives power. Knowledge of matters technical and professional and knowledge of the mechanics and systems of running the business.

Expertise is admirable and powerful. It comes from a combination of knowledge and experience, skilfully used and skilfully blended. Expertise is not easy to identify and value, and the manager who hides his light under a bushel is going to be undervalued. It is no use expecting to be esteemed unless you are prepared to assert your own expertise.

Behaviour which is seen to be that of a powerful and influential manager commands respect. It helps to earn power and influence.

The things which are seen to be influential in this sense vary from one enterprise to another. In one, that which is estimable may be equality, co-partnership, consultation, being seen to be concerned about subordinates and being seen to participate in their interests and activities. In a different enterprise, the influential are remote from the common herd: any descent from this level can positively reduce one's influence.

Doing favours. One of the most powerful "firms" in the world is said to be the Mafia, and part of the Mafia management process is said to be the trading of favours. If you do me a favour, I have a bounden duty to do one for you. Business is not like the Mafia, we hope, but the favour-system is.

Generosity. Your influence will be resisted if you try to keep all the interesting roles, responsibilities and authority to yourself. You will, of course, naturally want to retain what you can in order to have that fun which is an essential ingredient of managing. But if everything you do is at the expense of your colleagues and their fun, you will soon find yourself battling against powerful opposition. Once again, you have to get the balance right.

There are two other sources which give a person power and influence in the short term, but which are at the expense of long-term influence.

Immediacy. A person whose activities are essential for today's work is in a powerful position. If the caretaker alone can open the factory gates, then the caretaker has such immediacy that the place would stop without him. The caretaker has a very powerful key – in the short term.

But immediacy is menial. If the caretaker aspires to greater heights, he has to move into roles different from that of caretaker – roles in which his actions will influence events over a period of years rather than over a period of hours.

Replaceability. This is another variable in the power line-up. If you can leave tomorrow, and your successor be in control of events the day after, then you are easily replaceable. If it would take months and years to find anybody else who could take over your role, you are virtually irreplaceable (and therefore powerful) in the short term.

But in the long term, unless you move from your present role to a more important one, you will not earn the additional authority of a more senior position. Immediacy and irreplaceability give short-term power at long-term cost.

To summarise, power and influence are not entirely a matter of the formal authority which is vested in a manager. They are also a product of:

● His readiness to negotiate power and influence with his colleagues.

- His moving towards a central position.
- His being widely visible, out-and-about.
- His behaving in estimable ways.
- Being well informed about what is going on – both formally and informally.
- His knowledge of methods and systems.
- His expertise and his own valuation of that expertise.
- His generosity.

He could in the short term increase his power by hanging on to responsibilities which make him immediately hold a key to short-term activities, or by making himself irreplaceable: but either is at the cost of his long-term development.

Action Dos and Don'ts

DO
- Recognise that you can negotiate for more power.
- Recognise that there are plenty of other positive ways in which you can increase your influence.
- Decide precisely how to use those possibilities.

DON'T
- Assume that it is all up to "them".
- Waste your energy complaining.

DO
- Work positively to improve your position.

14 Self-organisation

This chapter will be different in form from the majority of the others. It is a chapter of hints for managers who feel that events press heavily on them.

Many people have the sense that they have too much to do, that constant pressures are working on them, that maybe they are failing to do something important. They feel lost within the surrounding haze, possibly trapped, uncertain and worried about it.

This chapter will make suggestions in the following sequence:

- First, let's clarify the problem.
- Then let's develop a technique for organising ourselves.
- Let's also develop techniques for problem-solving.
- Finally, let's keep control of events.

The problem

Numerous problems face us when we try to use our time effectively. Many of them are imposed on us from the outside. We all know about such problems:

● *The tyranny of the telephone.* It rings. It interrupts our concentration, and some idiot blathers on interminably.

● *Meetings.* We know meetings are essential. Still we cannot avoid the belief that there seem to be too many of them and they take too much time.

● *Interruptions.* Constantly there are people who want to see us, and some of us want to be known as having an ever-open door.

● *Work colleagues.* Perfectly rightly and properly, colleagues constantly look to us for help and support. We need positively to encourage them and ourselves to keep up the good relationships.

These problems are imposed on us, they make it difficult for us to set our priorities in order and to sustain our concentration on the key issues. One gets into a muddle. One is conscious that there is this mass of pressures and that amongst them there may be some, even more urgent, which are at present failing to get our attention.

The problem at this point is not simply this weight of pressures to act. It is, more seriously, the ambiguity in one's own mind. What is it that lies in this press of activities that is not being undertaken at the moment? Unless we can clarify that point, the uncertainty will continue to cause us stress and it will make matters worse.

Self-planning

In looking for tools to organise oneself better, first recognise that the 80/20 rule operates: 80 per cent of one's time is inevitably consumed by the imposed problems. By all means let us increase our efficiency in controlling those imposed problems – there are a few hints in the section on "Keeping Control" below – but we still find that a great deal of our time is taken up by outside pressures. For the sake of simplicity, let us continue to refer to it as 80 per cent.

The key to the effectiveness of our self-organisation is in the way we use the remaining 20 per cent.

This should be time used effectively to deal with today's priorities. It should also be time used to pave the way for a better tomorrow. Today's 20 per cent should influence the sort of thing we will have to deal with for 80 per cent of our time next year.

The planning tools we need are therefore those which will help us properly to control the 20 per cent of our time which is not commanded by imposed problems.

The approach we recommend for this self-planning comes in three stages.

1. Make an inventory of the activities which we might undertake in the next period. List all those pressures which surround us and which we think are demanding attention.

    ● Keep it simple.
    ● Do not try to be orderly.
    ● Jot at random.
    ● Do it quickly.

2. State priorities. Tackle this "prioritising" in whatever way suits you best. Some people like to start with a nice clean sheet of paper, neatly ruled with, say, four columns representing different priorities. The present writer goes about it more simply: he uses the priority rankings A = high, B = medium, C = low.

    He may re-classify one category – for example, the B category into B+, B and B–.

3. Set the high priority items into a work-plan: and list separately the lower priority items which cannot come into that plan and which must be held over for a later time.

For effective self-organisation there need to be several such work-plans of types to be discussed in the next section. The outcome of all these plans is different in form: but the process of producing them is consistently the same. To summarise:

● Make an inventory of possibilities.
● Set priorities.
● Plan.

Time scales

The authors use three time scales in planning their disposable work time. It may be that your situation is different: that you as a person will tend to operate differently, or that your job is such that our time spans are not the right ones for you. For example, the sort of detail in which we plan on a week-to-week basis might better suit you if you use it on a day-to-day basis or, at the other extreme, on a month-to-month basis. Decide for yourself which best suits you and do not feel that you should slavishly follow us.

The three different time scales for our self planning are:

● Annually.
● Quarterly.
● Weekly.

Annually, the planning takes two forms: a job review and a career review.

The job review relates to the long-term evolution of the job: it is looking at the grand design: for example, at the four fields into which this book is divided – Fun, Results, Ability to Achieve and Direction. It is concerned with the balance between those fields, and with the needs and opportunities for development amongst them.

The career review is concerned with one's own development, as distinct from the job's development. In what directions should I be developing my knowledge, ability, skill, experience? What steps should I be taking, with whom, to foster that result? More on self-development in Chapter 17.

The *quarterly* review is our own adaptation of the management-by-objectives formula. We do not use elegant forms for this, but a simple sheet of paper in which we set out three or four key result areas.

In each area we list two or three specific standards or targets that we will aim to have achieved by the end of the quarter. These are stated so far as possible in ways which can later be evaluated. For example, not "visiting as many customers as possible", but "visiting thirty-two customers".

The key result areas may be entirely work-centred, or one of them may be self-centred (relating to one's personal development).

Weekly, usually first thing on Monday morning, we develop the week's plan: the inventory of things we would like to get done this week, the choice amongst them of the priorities, the setting of the urgent matters into some schedule.

Our way of doing this is again more practical than elegant. Rule a sheet of paper into six columns, five of them for working days and the sixth headed CF (for carried forward). Insert in pen firm commitments – meetings and other appointments – then insert in pencil the time at which you will handle the priority tasks from your inventory. An example appears on p. 128.

Be realistic about it. Recognise that imposed problems will take much of your time. Make reasonable assumptions about the time for each of the special tasks that you want to do.

Keep this week-plan handy, and as you have a moment to spare, concentrate on the priority items.

The results of this particular planning are satisfying. Of course, we do not achieve precisely what we expect, precisely in the way planned, but it is remarkable to find at the end of the week that we can put a pen through most of our pencil plans, having managed to accomplish them.

We find too that the ambiguous cloud of other issues

which would otherwise weigh on us does not bother us. We had thought about the matter clearly on Monday morning. We had sensibly recognised what would have to be left over until next week, and we were able to give our undivided attention in brief spells to the most important issues.

MON	TUES	WED	THURS	FRI	C/F
Planning (Corresp.) 10.00 Salary Review Meeting ↓	I N T E R V I E W S	*(Corresp.)* *Annual Appraisals* *Prep. for London*	 9.30 D.o.T Committee 11.30 12.00 Philip ↓	J Birthday 9.00 Greenock Factory ↓	*Coaching/ Harry* *Paper for Victor* *Visits— – New – Derby – Oakden* *Office decoration*
JS Report: Prep. Monthly Stats. Prep. for I/Vs.	*(Corresp.) JS 1st Draft See M. Jock* NB: J's Birthday Present	 2.30 Ted KRAs *Find a Self Org. Seminar*	2.00 2.30 Hudsons ↓ 4.30	*(Corresp.) Prep. Monday Meeting (Trim Progs.)* *JS Final draft*	
		To London	Travel Home	Home Promptly (Theatre)	

Example of a week-plan. In this example typescript has been used for items normally inked in, manuscript for pencilled items

Incidentally, it is surprising how often the carried-forward items are carried forward not simply to next week, but to the week after and the week after. Finally they just vanish.

Those three plans – the annual, the quarterly and the weekly – are the basis on which we plan to use our time, both strategically and tactically.

Problem solving

Both in the 80 per cent of their time when managers are under imposed pressures, and in the 20 per cent which they should keep at their own discretion, they are likely to come up against problems, worrying situations where some action apparently needs to be taken.

Here are a couple of techniques we have found helpful, both for ourselves and in work with our clients, when faced with such worries.

Suppose that there is a problem because existing methods are not coping satisfactorily. Try following this sequence:

- Define the problem. First use random jottings about the problem; then on a separate sheet write down clearly – what the problem is.

   If you find that you need twenty words or more to express the problem, then you have not got your thinking clear enough. Try again.
- What are the causes? At random set down a list of causes of the problem.
- Analyse the causes under three headings:

   (*a*) It.
   (*b*) Them.
   (*c*) Me.

   It. Causes which derive from the hard facts – the procedures in use, the systems, the economic, technical or commercial factors.

   Them. Causes which relate to other people – those not here.

Me (or *Us*). Causes springing from my/our strengths and weaknesses, actions and inactions.

If analysis shows that there is a gross imbalance – and usually, at first sight, there are a lot more It and Them causes than Me causes – then you're not being honest with yourself. Try again.

● Action possibilities. Where have we leverage? What could we do? What are the possibilities?
● Intentions: what will who do?

That technique is often helpful when existing methods are not proving effective. A different technique is needed when a problem of a type we have not encountered before arises. It is then not a question of present methods not working, it is a question that we have no method at all.

The sequence to tackle this sort of problem is:

● What is the problem? Again accurate and simple definition is half the battle.
● What might we do? Be imaginative. Jot down possible solutions and possible lines of action and do not be afraid of setting down a few wild ideas. The imagination will be stifled if you worry about reality too much at this stage.
● What sensibly could we do? Choose two or three options which offer realistic scope for dealing with the problem.
● Evaluate, for each option the costs: money, time, other resources, relationships; and the consequences.
● Evaluate each consequence. We find it useful to draw an arrow to the right for a positive consequence, to the left for a negative. The length of the arrow indicates the strength of that consequence.
● Select and define action. A simple example of the technique is shown on p. 131.

Here then are a couple of bridges to problem-solving

to add to the battery of time-planning devices, annual, quarterly, weekly.

PROBLEM:	Car not available for commuting next week
OPTIONS:	Train Bus Taxi Bike Cadge lifts Hire car Borrow car Company car-port
BEST BETS:	Train Bus Cadge lifts

Problem-solving: listing the options

PROBLEM: Commuting next week

EVALUATION:

	TRAIN		BUS		CADGE LIFT	
	−	+	−	+	−	+
TIME	←		←			→
FLEXIBILITY		→		→	←	
INDEPENDENCE		→		→	←	
COST	←		←			→

Problem-solving: evaluation

Keeping control

The discipline of planning the 20 per cent of one's time which one can control is sufficient to remove much of the stress one feels when matters are more hazy. The problem is, of course, that it is all too easy to let this discipline lapse. At the least, one should have diary entries of the dates at which one will make the annual and the quarterly reviews.

The annual review is one document to be taken into account when making quarterly plans, and the quarterly plan should be checked periodically when preparing weekly plans.

When the time comes for conducting the next review, annual, quarterly or weekly, it should, of course, start with a check on one's effectiveness since the last review, not forgetting matters carried forward from that plan because they were not of sufficient priority at that time. Nor forgetting any high priorities which somehow were not done in time.

Fortunately, in our experience, these are rare. Once one is used to practising this sort of system, one's planning becomes reasonably accurate.

Other steps have to be taken to control the imposed pressures which we are supposing to command 80 per cent of our time.

In theory, we should be able to have incoming telephone calls filtered by the switchboard. Interruptions by visitors and colleagues are more difficult to avoid. If somebody takes the trouble to come to see us, then mere courtesy demands that we at least give them our attention, however briefly. Some balance must be struck to enable us to sustain and continue our communications, to encourage them, yet also to ensure that we do get 20 per cent of our time which we can dispose of according to our own priorities.

If you find yourself continuously trapped by the telephone and by other interruptions, then you have to take steps to avoid the trap.

Go to some place where you will not be interrupted. Use the office of an absent colleague for a while, or go to the canteen or the library.

For effective self-organisation you must reserve to yourself a sufficient share of your working time, and must plan to make the most effective use of that limited time.

In this chapter we have concentrated on ways to make

productive that 20 per cent of our time we can most readily control. This self-organisation, we hope, will help you to keep your priorities straight.

Finally, a hint about personal planning devices. The weekly planning is a device we use individually, something we do for ourselves. On the other hand, we find it helpful – almost imperative – to talk through our quarterly and annual reviews with third parties. At most points in our careers we have been blessed with bosses with whom it is easy to talk about such matters, and who value the chance to participate in such discussions. At other times we have had trusted subordinates. At yet other times we have needed third parties, outsiders. Always, we've needed some help.

Action Dos and Don'ts

DO
- Set out the issues needing your attention and put priorities on them.
- Keep 20 per cent of your time free of imposed problems.
- Plan annually, quarterly and weekly to achieve your priorities.
- Use problem-solving techniques to handle worrying situations.

DON'T
- Let circumstances be your master.
- Let imposed problems command all your time.

DO
- Zealously guard 20 per cent of your time against imposed problems.

15 Personal Skills

In seeking results, a manager must influence other people. He is seen by them to behave in ways which increase or decrese his influence.

Such behaviour is usually spontaneous. For example, when talking with colleagues, he is not concerning himself with the way in which he is behaving. His concern is concentrated a little on the other person (looking to see whether he seems to be picking up the message), more on sorting out his own thinking as he tries to articulate it.

Too many managers find themselves in positions of responsibility without ever having had the chance to check and polish such personal skills. Below is a checklist of them.

- *Using words.* Basic grammar and vocabulary.
- *Using numbers.* The ability to count, calculate, budget, etc.

    Both this and the first skill – words – depend on having a basic education and training; but the subsequent group can be developed during mid-career.

- *Oral presentation.* The ability to put across ideas on one's feet or sitting around a meeting table.
- *Listening skills.* The capacity to concentrate, understand what someone else is saying and encourage them.
- *Written presentation.* The ability to construct letters or reports in an interesting and animated way.
- *Negotiating skills.* The ability to work with other people, to achieve solutions in the common interest.
- *Creativity.* Imagining, inventing, developing, adapting.
- *Being helpful.* Listening and developing a rapport; conveying warmth, understanding, support; raising other people's self-esteem.
- *Leadership.* Beginning new tasks, ideas, projects. Leading and directing other people.
- *Follow through.* Ensuring that projects are followed through. Sustaining commitment when problems arise. And even being ready to recognise when the time has come to dismiss an unsuitable subordinate.

Examples

Nils-Erik Berg was a senior engineer working in the quality control department of a large Swedish mechanical engineering plant. He was very good with words and figures, he had a logical analytical mind, and he was the sort of leader who likes to be up front. He was reasonably creative and good at follow-up.

However, Nils-Erik was very low on intuition and helpfulness. His colleagues couldn't stand him.

When there was an opening for a manager in the quality control department, many people thought that Nils-Erik was technically the best-qualified person for the job but that he would be impossible to work with.

I was travelling home in an inter-city train one night recently when a friend – a distinguished professor of medicine in an important provincial university – happened to drop into the next seat. He'd had to run to catch the train, he was out of breath and out of temper. "Been to a council meeting", he said. "Had to get up early this morning and travel four hours journey to London, other people flying in from even further away.

"The items that we wanted to talk about had been pushed down the agenda. The chairman encouraged so much discussion on the first two items that the important things didn't come up until we were due to have finished.

"It has been an utter bloody waste of time. Four hours to get there. Long and tedious meeting. Now four hours more to get home. Ye gods, let's have a whisky!"

It took three for him to recover his normal cheerful equilibrium.

We all know examples of other people who need help with their personal skills.

An engineer, having carried out a project skilfully and promptly, has to write a report on the assignment. He sits down, sweats, worries and burns the midnight oil for nights on end.

The result is no more satisfactory to him than it is to his boss or would be to his clients. Other people have to go over it, rewrite it.

Inefficient for the organisation. Depressing and frustrating for the chap.

The manager who suddenly finds himself having to select staff. No training for the sort of characteristics which he should be on the lookout for. No skill in eliciting information. No ability to project a positive image of himself or of his company.

The boss calling his subordinates in for a meeting, imposing his ideas on them, giving them the impression that their own ideas and suggestions are unimpressive, even unwanted. Demotivating.

The experienced manager called on to present a paper at a conference. Recognising the honour, he spends ages drafting and redrafting the paper.

The outcome of the drafting too often is a superb coverage of the technology of the matter, put together in ways which are incomprehensible, presented with boring and demeaning diffidence.

The specialist pulled into a major negotiating team. Maybe anticipating hostile tactics and unwittingly creating a warlike atmosphere.

Or else, recognising a point of difference between the parties and too quickly suggesting a compromise.

The chap who talks interminably on the telephone.

The manager with the art of telling people what he wants.
   But who never listens.

Developing personal skills

The first example above was that of Nils-Erik Berg, the gifted technician. In actual practice, the consultant handling the assignment suggested that Nils-Erik would be the best man for the job if he could develop his personal skills. The MD of the operations said: "Prove he can do that, and he will get the job."

The consultant interviewed twenty people who knew Nils-Erik, and based on these interviews he designed a one-week crash course for him. It included both a little technical training and a lot of personal skill development.

During this week Nils-Erik was engaged every day from 8 a.m. until 2 a.m. the next morning. The days and nights were full of activity, always at least two consultants (one psychologist and one engineer) working with him, lecturing and role-playing.

During the first two days he was given a tough time, and he learnt for the first time in his life that other people saw him as an unpleasant person – but that he could do something about it. Through massive feedback during the week, Nils-Erik changed dramatically. This was the first time in his life that he really received any feedback, and he used it very positively.

He went home a new man, and he was given the job.

A couple of weeks later, there was a flood of calls to the company. People in different positions asked: "What have you done to Nils-Erik? He is completely different – for the better."

As we have been able to check, Nils-Erik has sustained this new level of personal skills for almost ten years, and he is now on the board of directors in the company.

The other examples are all of defective personal skills.

Very few people are born with natural talents in these personal skills, just as very few people are born with natural talents to be brilliant footballers or superb swimmers.

For most of us, not so naturally gifted, there is a need to develop the skills. This is not simply a matter of knowledge. You can read all the books you like, but you will never be able to swim until you have been in the water.

We can offer guidelines – we give some below – but they are no substitute for practice under controlled conditions with plenty of feedback.

In principle, there are consistent guidelines for conduct of all the personal skills. They need to be refined in detail for each, but the main common elements are:

- *Preparing.* Organising one's thinking to become simple and clear.
- *Externalising.* Concentrating one's energy on the other party or parties. Letting that energy permeate the communication.
- *Structuring.* Organising the pattern of communication into a few sharp and simple sections.

● *Non-verbalising.* Using the battery of non-verbal communications: eye contact, posture, gesture, animation, visual aid.

These are brief guidelines. They need much development, but even so they can only be guidelines. They are no substitute for trying, testing and polishing one's abilities under controlled conditions.

	Poor	Barely adequate	Average	Good	Very good	Excellent
Using words						
Using numbers						
Oral presentation						
Listening skills						
Written presentation						
Chairmanship						
Negotiating skills						
Creativity						
Being helpful						
Leadership						
Follow through						
Profile of personal skills						

To help you review your own personal skills we present the checklist of personal skills again here, this time in a form which will help you to do a little personal checking. We suggest that you make three or four photocopies of the form; complete one form to show a profile of your own skills; and ask two or three colleagues each to prepare their separate estimate of your profile. You will find two things: one is useful information for yourself; the other is that your colleagues will want some extra blank photocopies!

Action Dos and Don'ts

DO
● Recognise that you have instinctive behaviour which can make or mar your ability to produce results.
● Check whether there is scope to polish behaviour.
● Get help in the polishing.

DON'T
● Assume that you are none of the miscreants in the examples.

DO
● Treat yourself to a chance to polish your personal skills.

16 Adapting to One's Customers

Who are your customers?
What do they want?
How do you serve them?
How do you keep in touch with them?

First, who are your customers? Not your company's customers, but your own "customers" – the people for whom you produce things or to whom you give advice or service.

If you do not know who your customers are, then you are unlikely to be giving them the sort of service they want.

They certainly include your boss. He pays.

They include the managers to whom your output goes.

They include the people upstairs who are responsible for deciding your fate.

And they include those who in any way contribute to your performance.

Unless you satisfy all these sorts of customer, you will not reach a position from which to produce results.

Examples

Stan King and *John Goldman* worked well together. Stan had tremendous strengths in being able to look at a whole range of different things going on around the company, and creatively find ways of putting them into new ideas, new developments. Stan too was very good at analysing those ideas, seeing the sort of actions that were needed.

Stan produced excellent papers. Trouble was, nobody was enthused by writing. That is where John proved brilliant. Nowhere near as good in his original thinking as Stan, he yet had the capacity to talk and to convey enthusiasm. Together Stan and John produced remarkable results. They were not of the elegant excellence for which Stan longed, but they did happen, they were profitable, the customers were satisfied.

Tom Wilson was a computer manager, also brilliant. At least, we all thought so. We frankly did not quite understand what was going on in the black box, but we believed that it had enormous potential for us. Somehow or other we needed to know more about it, and then, we thought, Tom would be able to help us greatly.

Our internal telephone directory was on a sheet of card. Most of us had cards worn and dog-eared over a period of time, with amendments scribbled over the original printing.

Tom had the idea of producing something very much better. He programmed the computer to produce a new list. It could be analysed by surnames, or by titles of department, or by numerical order. It could be updated instantly. The new telephone list was excellent in a way in which our old card was awful.

It was distributed from a computer print-out; the product was a sheet 8 inches wide and nearly 5 feet long, with innumerable folds in it. Most of us were unable to find our way round this excellent new directory and quickly went back to using our old cards.

Somehow or other Tom's apparent excellence never earned the kudos some people thought he merited. Frankly, he never overcame the handicap of that telephone directory invention and vanished from the company a few months later. He might have been a good man, but his delivery system let him down.

Airlines provide some excellent examples of marketing and of mis-marketing. Despite the outrageous prices charged by European airlines (on international comparisons per mile flown), the service is usually poor.

SAS in 1982 gave their customers an extra couple of inches leg-room, printed elegant menus, and the cabin staff began to cosset their passengers in a new way. Suddenly it was no longer a misery to have to travel SAS.

Anybody travelling from London to Edinburgh during 1983 had the option of flying British Airways or British Midland. Both delivered the same basic service, taking the passenger from point A to point B; but there was a vast difference in secondary service. BM's provision of meals, drinks and customer service was massively better. Given the same fares, it is obvious that BM would attract the customer instead of BA.

BM had a better "service delivery system".

Analysis

Satisfying your customers depends on meeting their needs and their wants. No two customers are identical, but most have collective needs and wants as well as individual ones.

Competent marketing to our customers hangs on finding out what are their wants, in what ways are they satisfied and in what ways are they disappointed with our output. It is simple, straightforward market research. Tom Wilson, the computer manager, bungled it.

What do we give our customers? Most of us who are interested in our jobs want to produce an excellent product or give an excellent service. It is fun for us to develop our products towards that concept of excellence. But that is our fun. It is not necessarily our customers' satisfaction. A pity that Tom missed the point.

What about packaging? Some customers are concerned about the quality of the product or of the idea which we produce for them. Others are more concerned about what it looks like. A splendidly packaged product or idea – one which is beautifully presented – will win accolades from one sort of customer. A different customer will find it wasteful and be much more critical of the contents.

It was the idea of the service delivery system which lay behind SAS developing a new attraction for their customers. This is part of thinking developed recently in Scandinavia which says:

- You must have a product or a service which people want. Find out what they want.
- You must deliver it in a way which they find appealing. In the airline case, a little more legroom, better food and drink, better and more service, a happier and more welcoming smile.
- Create a good image. Create it through your product, through the way it is delivered, and through your publicity to make sure that it is known and recognised.
- This will stimulate market demand; and market demand will influence you to redesign your product. So the cycle starts all over again.

This cycle – product, delivery, image, demand – must at all stages be consistent with your own character and with that of your firm. It must be consistent with your business idea and with the things you value. The concept is shown diagrammatically below.

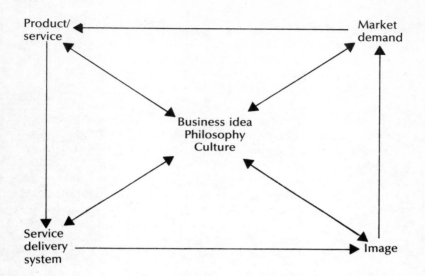

The service management system

Action Dos and Don'ts

DO
- Write out a list of your customers.
- Check what they want, need, find satisfying.
- Tailor your output and your service delivery system to meet their expectations.
- Keep regular contact with your customers.

DON'T
- Proceed without checking what your customers want.

DO
- Check your service delivery system.

SUMMARY OF PART 3

The Ability to Achieve a position of influence is one of the key fields for any manager's endeavour.

If he is to have the best chance to perform, he needs to work within a culture which complements his own abilities. He needs to develop the best possible relationship with his boss, and to seek other patronage. He has to have competent subordinates and he has to "sell" his position to those around him.

A sense of timing is vital. It is helpful to remember that both people and events ripen, and the opportunity of ripeness needs to be seized.

Colleagues influence our ability to achieve a position from which we can perform. The positive manager is constantly polishing his relations with others and trying to make the most of people's differing talents.

Power and influence are not entirely a matter of the formal authority vested in a manager. Chapter 13 suggested half a dozen different ways of building influence: "centrality", "out-and-about" character, estimable behaviour, the building of information, knowledge, expertise and generosity.

Self-organisation is important if one is to be influential. It is no use living in a haze of ambiguity and uncertainty, constantly reacting to immediate pressures. Recognise that you must protect 20 per cent of your time and that you must impose your own priorities on that 20 per cent.

You will only succeed if you have sufficient personal skills, in using words and numbers, speaking, writing and negotiating; in creating and helping, and leading and following through.

Finally, Chapter 16 has emphasised the need to adapt to the requirements of one's "customers", to sustain their allegiance and to meet their needs.

To be a good manager you have to balance your effort over all those forces.

Part 4

DIRECTION

HEADING IN THE RIGHT DIRECTION

INTRODUCTION TO PART 4

All the effort you put into making your job enjoyable, producing results and achieving influence is counter-productive unless you are trying to ensure that the right things are done. You have to be heading in the right direction.

That is the theme of the final part of this book, which will form the following sequence:

- *Personal goals*. Focusing your own visions, hopes and aspirations for your work and for yourself.
- *Group goals*. Identifying the corresponding hopes and aspirations of your work-group and of your employers.
- *Strategy*. The headlines of the grand design which will enable you to move towards your personal and group goals.
- *Target-setting*. Planning a measured pace and setting milestones for your pursuit of the strategy.
- *Shepherding*. Ensuring that the strategy is implemented, the targets met.
- *The art of the possible*. Accepting that it is no use pursuing the impossible.
- *Changing direction*. The process of changing established practices and strategies.

17 Personal Goals

Personal goals come in three categories: task-centred, job-centred and self-centred.

Each of us has some task-centred goal, something one longs to achieve in one's work. Maybe it is to carry through some treasured project, to introduce some new system, to replace some outdated equipment, or to influence the way in which one's team operates. All are instances of task-centred personal goals.

We can also have job-centred personal goals. We may want to make our jobs more enjoyable, more challenging or more influential.

The third type of personal goal is that which is self-centred. Such goals may take the form of developing our abilities – enhancing our training or our experience – or of taking steps to see our abilities are put to better use.

Examples

Herbert Johnson, the cashier who moved up eventually to become managing director, had clear personal goals for his work.

He valued financial expertise and believed that it should have an even more significant influence on the affairs of his company. He valued too his personal influence in the firm and drew satisfaction from using and extending that influence.

He had clear personal goals.

Alan Griffiths was a different type of person. Much less restless and ambitious, he valued his security. He was a work study manager and his progress was good if never inspiring. Under encouraging leadership, he took on considerable responsibility.

One day his company was taken over. Six months later it had become obvious that neither Alan's star nor that of his boss was any longer in the ascendant. His boss quietly told Alan that he was about to leave, and he arranged that Alan be offered an appointment of reasonable status in another company.

Alan didn't take it. Safety and security in the known job and with the known pension rights ranked higher than adventure in Alan's values in his mid-forties.

That story does not end there. Five years later, now almost fifty, Alan was made redundant. Suddenly venturesome, he emigrated and took a job abroad in an expanding organisation. He now flourished as he had not done during the previous five years. It took the redundancy to force Alan out of his safety mould into new growth.

Arne Rud, on the other hand, is a great career planner. He has divided his life into three-year periods, the ultimate goal being to become a professor of industrial management at thirty-five. Not only that, he aspires to a specific chair from which the present professor is going to retire at a predictable time.

Arne took his doctorate (of course on time) in business administration. He planned then to spend three years learning the politics of Scandinavian working life, and took a job in the central administration of a trade union. Although he greatly enjoyed his job, he left after the exact time and went on to be a consultant with a logistics firm, in order to broaden his experience. This also was pre-planned.

His next step was to become a production director for a fairly big steel mill, building experience of production management for three years. And having learned this new trade, he went on to his present job with a computer firm, selling systems, adding both marketing and selling to his repertoire of experience. Today he has one year left in that company.

At the same time Arne has been writing papers and tutoring researchers at the university in question, thus preparing the ground on the academic side. The present professor is going to retire in two years' time, so Arne is going to miss his twelve-year journey by one year. There is presently no serious competition for the chair: Arne is going to make it. And he has been having fun all the way.

Here are some examples of people following different development paths at different ages.

Elaine Cunningham and *Frank Rennie* left university at the same time. Both of them had respectable degrees and both had played an active part in undergraduate society. Each of them had been an officer in a club and had had a success record.

Elaine joined a company which believed in challenging its people. Within a week she found she was off on a work-study course. Three weeks later she was at an outpost of her company, challenged to introduce a more effective way of assembling cartridges. That wasn't too difficult. Some simple applications of time and motion study techniques soon showed what was wrong. What was difficult was convincing the staff that there might be a better way, winning the commitment of the supervisors and the departmental manager, coping with the anxiety of a union area secretary keen to find some opportunity to enhance his standing with his members. That is what really took the effort. But four months after she had left university, Elaine had measured up to that challenge, had put the new method into operation, and was moving on to her next challenge.

Frank's story was quite different. He entered a local government authority as a management trainee with high promises of being on a career path towards top-level responsibility. He found himself employed in the education offices, where his main job was to draft advertisements for teachers. Since these advertisements were to a standard pattern which he could not seriously influence, it was pretty boring. It took but a fraction of his time. "I am supposed to be here for 7 hours a day. I have one hour's work to do and then I spend another hour trying to think of useful things that I might do and that manages to provide me with a little more occupation. But that still leaves several hours a day with nothing to do but chatter or read or do crosswords."

Three years later Elaine had grown and was taking more and more responsibility. Frank had stultified.

Camille Bonnevier and *Henry Grey* were both in their thirties, both capable people, both thought to have bright futures. When Camille left the Sorbonne, he (like Frank Rennie) went into local government, but was quickly bored and moved on to private industry. He changed jobs three times in the next six years, gained considerable experience, was fortunate enough to be given plenty of opportunity for personal development.

He joined a major group at a time when they were going in for a new product and needed to set up a new subsidiary company. As luck would have it, his name came on to the short list to set up the new subsidiary whilst he was still only thirty-two. It was a great challenge. He rose to it. He grew and the company grew with him.

Henry Grey spent all his working career with one employer and had become a factory manager by the time he was thirty-five. Spotlighted as a front runner for the future, he was sent off on a lengthy business school course and came back with a host of new ideas about how things should be done. Henry and those close to him now sought to optimise their methodology, but somehow nothing changed.

I have always wondered what would have happened if Henry had been given Camille's opportunity. And vice versa.

Lennart Berggren at the age of forty-five was working at the level just below the board of directors in a big commercial bank. He found life slightly boring and could see no vision of interesting opportunities around the corner in the banking sphere. Was this what life had intended for him?

He changed jobs and joined a consultancy organisation where he is working harder than ever. His family says that he is now looking and acting ten years younger.

David Searle at forty-five was working as staff training manager in a large pulp-making company. He had a charming, professional wife and three competent children, and his friends thought of him as successful.

David was not so satisfied. He felt that his professional development had probably reached its peak. He felt that life must have more to offer him, and he set out to explore new ways of enjoying himself. It caused a lot of distress in the family, and within a couple of years they had split up. David was living with someone else and had been to many group weekends which massaged his ego.

Two years later still, he was again painfully in the process of separating, this time from the second partner.

Golf clubs have many members who are much older than forty-five. It is noticeable that some men in their late fifties and sixties who have retired early and have little to do are withering. Others in their seventies remain active and still enjoy life.

Analysis

Herbert Johnson, ambitious and thrusting, had strong personal goals for his work. Those personal goals were consistent with the company's interest, and he took advantage of every opportunity to further them, to reach towards them.

Several of the anecdotes show the importance for personal development of being in a positive environment. Consider the changes in Alan Griffiths's succession of appointments; the difference between the development in Elaine and Frank, the difference between Camille and Henry.

Much of any manager's development takes place without strong conscious effort. It takes place as he works on his job, building new experiences, seeing people at work, making a few mistakes but accomplishing a great deal.

In that critical on-the-job development there is nothing to touch the luck of having a good boss. The experience, example, help and impulses from such a boss are priceless.

There are other sorts of on-the-job development. In the nursing profession, for example, there is the practice of "acting up" (taking over more senior responsibilities for a limited time).

Another device is the use of project work: having to achieve some specific result within a specified time. To be effective for personal development, this demands not simply the taking of decisions but the management of a process or project from its infancy until it is tried, tested and proven.

And of course there is training. Training by doing, under close supervision and instruction; or off-the-job in courses, seminars or private study.

The need for personal development changes as one matures. From the cradle to the grave there is a consistent sequence of development for all mankind. Roughly, it is possible to set ages to that sequence and to attune one's career development to it.

In our twenties we tend to be highly adventurous. Much of our lives to date has been taken up by acquiring qualifications. We now come to an age at which we expect those qualifications to be rewarded both with interesting work and with the good things of life; but we find ourselves at a disadvantage because an older generation respects experience, which they see us as lacking.

It pays us then to gain experience fast. Project work is the best form of compressed experience.

In our thirties we have new roots. We tend towards higher stability (fewer job changes) in our working life. In our domestic lives we have been growing roots – home, spouse, children. We devote quite a lot of energy to building relationships and establishing the foundation for an old-boy network.

Intellectually we are more rational (relatively less emotional) than ever before or after.

Our energy remains high and we have grafted experience on to our qualifications. We are at our fittest for pioneering, energetic and developmental management. This is the time to build our personal skills to complement our knowledge, experience and energy.

In our forties we start with the same zest, but gradually life changes. The dear children grow into "bloody teenagers". Our careers, which previously seemed to have limitless horizons, may now be seen to be bounded – no longer is it reasonable to think that we might aspire to the key role in a major enterprise . . . maybe not even beyond our present job.

This period in our lives is sometimes called the mid-life crisis. The way we cope with it is important. If we accept the changes and if we adjust (like Arne Rud), we can develop a new and satisfactory life-style. If we resist, trying exaggeratedly to sustain the attitudes and behaviour of our younger selves, we're likely to overdo things, like David Searle.

In our fifties work takes less importance in our priorities. For most of us, the glamour, the zest, the commitment are of a different order. Our ability to contribute has also changed: our strengths now are our experience and our stability where before they were our energy, imagination, creativity.

This sequence of personal development will apply to most readers of this book. The precise timing may, of course, vary: some of us grow old before our time, others retain the characteristics of a period beyond their normal span. Part of our ability to retain our vitality depends on our enjoying our work and on our positioning. If we have managed well in those directions, we will have worked in a stimulating milieu. We will have had plenty of opportunity and challenge, to which we will have responded to our satisfaction and to the benefit of our personal development. But if we're stagnating without adequate attention to enjoyment and positioning, we will soon wither.

Our personal goals should therefore take account of the natural biological development we can all expect during successive stages of our careers.

It is all very well to talk of setting such personal goals, but life development is also a question of opportunity, of the chances which present themselves. In the course of our work we meet many people whose talents seem to us to be out of balance with their responsibilities: apparently capable people whose strengths are not being exploited; or the opposite, people who have achieved positions of status which they don't seem to justify.

As we try to rationalise such evidence, we are struck repeatedly by the role luck has played in their development. The happy chance of being in the right place, knowing the right person, seizing an opportunity at the right time.

Or not seizing it.

The readiness to grasp opportunities is partly a personal matter of risk-taking. Some of us have a high concern for the security of our jobs. Others of us have a higher readiness — even urge — to be venturesome, to exploit new chances, to take new roles.

Each of us operates within the bounds of his own nature and of the opportunities we perceive. Each needs to get his thinking clear about his personal goals, and thereby ready himself to seize (or not to seize) opportunities. Maybe even to create them.

Action Dos and Don'ts

DO
- Crystallise your visions for your work-place.
- Set yourself challenging goals in pursuit of your vision.
- Set yourself a personal development programme.
- Recognise that your strengths will change as you move through your career.

DON'T
- Expect to have security and growth in equal measures.
- Expect too much of the real world.

DO
- Be ready to seize opportunities.

18   Group Goals

Personal goals are important for a manager. He should take them into account in deciding the direction in which he wants to move.

But personal goals are only a part of the picture. The interests of the enterprise *and* the interest of one's work-group should have more powerful influence.

With his boss, with his colleagues, and with the people who work for him, the manager will be engaged in constant dialogue, and together they should have visions of what they want to achieve. Balancing the possible with the desirable, seeking for common commitment, checking timing and ripeness, the group goals have to be narrowed down. It is no use finding yourself over-extended. Concentrate.

Traditional thinking has emphasised "strategic planning" or "corporate planning". Both have been taken to imply some major forecasting of political, economic, technical and even social trends, leading to the production of intricate plans for some lengthy period – maybe five years.

Such grand strategies condition the plans for the whole of an enterprise and imply a process of developing and goal-setting in each part of it. Conventional theory is that this system should tell you your group goals.

There is plenty of contrary opinion. Many people who have tried hard to plan on those lines have given up, finding such strategies were simply paper-producing exercises, demanding much effort and based on too many assumptions. Often the assumptions are disproved by events, and recent theory suggests a quite different approach.

Examples

John Goldman had a personal vision of people at work in ways which they found challenging and enjoyable. This personal vision was compatible with the group goals within which he was expected to work. His work-group aimed to spread the influence of Personnel and to give people every opportunity to be effective. There were plenty of places in his group which were not ripe for any sort of movement. Strategy for John was therefore to concentrate his effort mainly on factories ripe for a change in their personnel practices. This meant that he influenced the ways in which people were trained, recruited, selected. He looked at the personnel systems in each factory and made sure that they were regularly reviewed. He checked on the structures and made sure that personnel representatives had adequate access to line management, and that their activities were fully integrated into the local works. He was particularly concerned with the quality of personnel staff and with their skills.

By contrast, *Ole Johansen* was the bright and energetic

accountant brought into a large but decaying organisation. His sponsors brought him in because they were
confident that he could revitalise the organisation.

Trying energetically to introduce new methods and to
influence people working in set patterns – many of them
elderly and inflexible people – Ole was constantly
frustrated. His sponsors had not taken any other major
steps to revive the organisation, and after a couple of
years Ole (with little achievement behind him) was busy
looking for a new job.

Madeleine Andersson was running a subsidiary of a large
food company. There were twelve such subsidiary companies, and when Madeleine took over the 2,500
employees in her company it rated No. 11 on performance.

Madeleine was ambitious and determined that her
company should out-perform the other subsidiaries. Her
idea was to become heavily customer-oriented, and to
win an increasing share of the market. In pursuit of those
goals she broke her company down into twenty separate
profit centres, encouraging entrepreneurship in each of
the respective managers. She arranged a special
customer service course for all sales and distribution
staff.

She changed the leadership style. Whereas before it
had been a remote "management by memo", now it
became the more personal "management by walking
around". She personally ensured that this style spread at
least as far as 100 first-line supervisors.

The team reviewed a whole range of systems and
work-flow from purchase to delivery with the rallying
call: "Close to the Customers".

Within eighteen months, company performance
shifted from No. 11 to No. 2 amongst the subsidiary
companies. The No. 1 subsidiary has a particularly
privileged market position, but Madeleine is closing in.

Analysis

The examples illustrate the range of activity which successful managers must take into account in setting their group goals. This range has been put in a new way in one of the most exciting books in recent management literature, Thomas J. Peters' and Robert Waterman's *In Search of Excellence*.

The essense of their doctrine is threefold:

- The manager cannot always control everything.
- There is a range of activities which must be harmonised for the efficient conduct of any business.
- Seek not for perfection but strive to ensure that those activities all lead towards the same goal, and make it possible for them to head that way.

The variables which Peters and Waterman describe are:

- Shared values – the binding force which has to exist before people and things are working solidly together; people having a common binding vision.
- Structure – the pattern of organisation.
- Systems – processes, procedures, controls of the organisation.
- Strategy – the broad direction in which the organisation is aiming to move.
- Skills – the ability of people and of the organisation to carry out their tasks ("The Skill of X to produce Y").
- Staff – the people; their innate quality and the means to increase that innate quality.
- Style – the way in which the enterprise functions.

Peters and Waterman studied a range of companies whose performance was excellent by any standards. The companies worked in very different ways, yet all produced excellent results. The common factor was that the seven Ss (listed above) worked in harmony. They pulled in the same direction.

You may, for example, have a company with an extremely authoritarian boss, one who is loved, hated and admired. He is the sort who unwittingly balances his Ss: his Style is implemented by a Structure which lets him exert influence in detail, and by a Staff who are scared stiff and behave according to his every whim. On the other hand, in a company with a democratic type of leader, his Structure will give maximum freedom to his Staff to create their own Strategy, to develop their own Systems and their own Skills.

In both cases you might find an excellent company measured in terms of financial success.

Peters and Waterman note eight other findings which mark excellent companies. We list them here and follow with explanatory notes about those which are not obvious:

- Focus on action and execution.
- Close to the customer/distributor.
- Productivity through people.
- Autonomy/entrepreneurship.
- Simple form, and lean staff.
- Stick to your knitting.
- Hands on, value driven.
- Simultaneous loose–tight properties.

"Autonomy/entrepreneurship" means that the company strives very hard to organise in a way that enables each manager really to influence his own results.

"Hands on" means that people get dirty fingers from really stretching to the benefit of the customers, be they internal "customers" or actual customers. "Value driven" means that they really believe in and act on their basic values. Such a rallying call as "we believe in people" would be a value firmly practised in excellent companies, but mere and meaningless words in ineffective ones.

"Simultaneous loose–tight properties" means that the companies apply very tight control on performance related to their basic values, but very loose, almost sloppy, control in other areas.

Finally, we would like to emphasise the fact that the

excellent companies do not all act the same way. They do not conform to any particular theory of business administration. "Nothing comes first", to use an expression from Peters and Waterman. Success comes from energetically ensuring that the seven Ss work in unison.

The examples in this chapter have included Ole's frustration when he was unable to shift the whole range of Ss in a different direction; and the successes of John and Madeleine in shifting all the Ss. Neither John nor Madeleine had ever heard of Tom Peters or Bob Waterman.

Action Dos and Don'ts

DO
- Look at your activities. Ask yourself which of the seven Ss you rate most highly and which of them now needs attention.
- Check that all seven are pulling in the same direction.
- Concentrate on the pair of Ss most imbalanced.

DON'T
- Sweat about perfection.
- Theorise too much.
- Waste energy on purely paper exercises.

DO
- See that everyone is heading in the same direction.

19 Strategy

Strategy is "a pretty clear idea about how I would like to defeat my competitors in the long term".

How long is long term?

It depends on the manager, his product(s) and his job. If you are the boss of a massive industrial empire, the long term is five or ten years away. If you are a first line supervisor, it is five or ten days ahead. For many middle managers it is about a year away.

Do we really need to worry about strategy? It all depends. If you are working in very stable conditions in which your customers (*your* customers – the people whom you personally have to serve with goods and services) are stable customers, your technology is stable, and the processes that you use are stable, then you will expect to go on doing the same sort of things as you have done in the past. You will no doubt want from time to time to change things a little – for example to improve some system or to change a little the way people are trained – but you will not be looking for any grand strategic change. Your great concern will be to use your increasing experience, keeping ahead of competitors in cost and service.

That is perfectly reasonable. That's how life is for many of us. There is no need for us to worry about the urgings of clever pundits who say we ought to change.

It is, of course, possible that we will be overtaken by catastrophe outside our control. The firm may close. But if we are tucked away in the middle of such a stable operation, there is nothing that we can do to change the grand strategy of the organisation – it is far too durable – and worrying isn't going to help.

There is nothing to be ashamed of in this. When the organisation needs routine, continuity, smoothness, then dramatic change is not appropriate. What is more, any sort of dramatic change so rocks the boat that all sorts of unexpected leaks suddenly start spouting up. A little change in the progress control means that production planning is exposed, found imperfect; and then the sales order system, having worked successfully for twenty years, is suddenly seen to be faulty.

Do not look for drastic change strategies in stable situations.

But in other situations, do worry about strategy. If you are conducting operations in which the technology is changing, in which you need to develop new "customers", or in which you need to innovate, then you need to do something dramatic.

Both for your own effectiveness, and for the effectiveness of the people around you, that dramatic development must be articulated. You've got to be able to say what you want to do.

Your strategy is the way you want to change things in the long term. Your strategy must be something you can follow tenaciously for that long term – something you will support and sustain for a year and more, if you are middle management. It is something that is going to take effort. If you are going to go on running your normal job, taking 80 per cent of your time, then the energy you will have available for strategic development is limited to 20 per cent of your work-time.

It may well take much more of your thinking and creative time. Positive thinkers lying in their baths or saunas think about strategies, not of the cares and concerns of routine. That means that they have a reasonable amount of time for strategic thinking; but of their operational time, they have at most 20 per cent available for strategic development.

One's ambitions for strategy development, therefore, must be restricted to one or two top priority plans.

Those plans must be so chosen that one has the competence and the influence to see them through. It is no use aiming for something if there are going to be insuperable obstacles.

Many forces have to be balanced in formulating strategy.

1. *Continuity/change.* There has to be a balance between our attention to continuity and our attention to change. We have so far talked about this balance in the simple language of the 80/20 rule – 80 per cent of activity to routine and 20 per cent to change; but life is not really so simple. Some of us are in jobs where little major change is appropriate: 90/10 might be a better balance. Others of us work in more dramatic situations, and may need, if we can, to devote 30 per cent or even 40 per cent of our time to strategic matters.

    How should you balance the amount of effort you put into keeping the wheels turning, and the amount you put into strategic development?

2. *Thinking/doing.* Thinkers think and doers do. And, by our observations, those who spend most time thinking often get least done.

    Does strategy have to be thought about very carefully? Not always. Some people have the ability to use the conscious part of their brains and to translate those thoughts into words. Others, and they are often highly successful people, have much more of an instinctive grasp of strategy, a feeling inside, one which is only disturbed by forcing them to rationalise and articulate the reasons for their strategy.

What matters most is having the ability to get on with it and see it through.

3. *Complexity/simplicity*. The rationale of strategies is very complex. The combination of personal and group goals, opportunities and ambitions, different interest groups and . . . . It is all very complicated.

But it must be said simply.

Strategies have to carry the commitment, the tenacity and the dedication of their sponsors.

You can't dedicate yourself to something you're not clear about. The more simply you can state it, the clearer you will be. And the clearer will be those whose help and support you want. Avis's "We try harder", is a great rallying call, as is "IBM means service", or Caterpillar's "24 hours spare-part service".

4. *Efficiency/effectiveness*. Efficiency is improving the way things are done in our own patch.

Effectiveness is the way in which that patch relates to surrounding people and things. We have to balance our attention to the two.

Too much concentration on efficiency – for instance, by cost-cutting – could mean that we create an organisation which can no longer relate to changing market conditions.

5. *Time needed/time available*. How much time are we to spend on developing our strategies? Well, there are about 220 working days in a year. Possibly 80 per cent of that time is needed to keep things running. That would leave us about forty days in which to plan.

Let's be generous and say that we only need half that forty for all the other things this book is telling us about. That leaves twenty for strategy.

Two days for deciding strategy, eighteen days' hard work to implement it. It won't be a period of eighteen days nicely separated from the routine days, of course. It will be odd moments planned well ahead, and opportunities grasped as they occur. Taken together, these moments can add up to maybe eighteen days a year. That's a rough idea of your time for strategic development.

6. *Consulting/deciding*. If we want commitment from other people, then we should consult them in the process of taking decisions about strategy; but that costs time and inevitably dilutes our decision.

On the other side of the equation, if we spend time together with people in the decision-making process, we don't need to spend time selling them the solution afterwards.

What is the balance for you?

Examples

Paul Wood, early in his industrial career, was given a project to carry out. It was a project we met before in Chapter 10: reviewing the progress control system. He was warned at the outset: "Whatever you decide to do, you will find it takes four months to have it in good running order, so you really need it installed pretty quickly."

Paul didn't find much difficulty in devising an improved progress control system. The old one had been in use for over fifteen years, it had been patched up from time to time and it was ripe for change.

Everybody recognised the need for change. The only blockage was a production manager who was renowned for being indecisive.

Paul hit on a simple strategy. He waited until that manager went on holiday and then worked hard. He sold his suggested new method to the managing director, to the deputy production manager, to supervisors and to the union. He pushed ahead urgently to the point at which the system was installed before the production manager came back from holiday. Installed, but not running smoothly. There were many teething troubles and Paul did indeed need four months' running-in time.

Surprisingly, he was much helped by the production

manager when he returned from holiday. We had guessed that the latter would feel that action had been taken behind his back and that he would be hostile. On the contrary, he was delighted to find that decisive action had been taken without his having to decide.

George Reid was the visionary with a remarkable ability to challenge and inspire people all around him. His own visions were focused far in the future, his strategies tried to ensure that his people would continue to enjoy the opportunity to perform in the light of changing markets which he saw threatening them. He was for ever thinking three or four years ahead and trying to position the company so that his people were satisfied, challenged, extended.

Jim Baldwin was the super salesman who was promoted to sales manager. He beavered away trying to expand sales, corresponding with agents, personally handling major accounts. Low in strategic thinking, low in change–orientation, slow to bring new methods and people.

Not entirely wrongly. The trade was a very stable one. It was not ripe for radical change; but somebody needed to be thinking about development of the company's markets and about what sort of products would be needed to satisfy them, and nobody was doing it. In the course of a decade his company's position gradually sagged until there came a court revolution. It was traumatic for everybody, not least for Jim, who left by mutual agreement when faced with new people and new methods which frankly were outside his range of experience and ability.

Derek Short, our charismatic leader with the tremendously strong personality, was a great doer. Full of ideas, he had the right instincts for business. He did not waste too much time in articulating them, but got on with them, and by energy and personality pulled the boat along behind him.

Herbert Johnson (cashier to managing director) proposed a new scheme for financial control, with profitability as the criterion for all companies and factories, right down to departmental level. Seductive as it sounds, this sytem had flaws, and it met a great deal of resistance both from managers and from more conservative accountants.

Herbert sold the idea upstairs. Pushed for it. Found the resistance growing. Kept on pushing. After two years there were still snags, loopholes, objections: there was a strong swell of opposition. But Herbert stuck to his guns, persuading, cajoling, working on the influential. He had the company accountant from one of the strongest objectors re-assigned to his own staff and replaced by one of his own people. The battle over "profitability control" went on and on. Anybody less fanatical would have given up after two or three years.

But Herbert was committed and dedicated. He stuck to his strategy. At last, after five years of battle, Herbert's proposal was suddenly appreciated. It happened that the company's markets became depressed and the "profitability control" tool was a key which helped the company to reorganise for the new situation. Herbert's perseverance with his strategy paid off, both for the company and for Herbert with his personal ambitions.

John Clegg took up his new appointment as managing director of a service company with 24,000 employees at a time when it was incurring heavy losses, the worst in the company's history.

The company was technically orientated; people loved the sophisticated machinery.

John saw a need to change from this technical orientation to a market orientation. One of his early and controversial comments was: "Our most valuable asset is a satisfied customer."

That became a cornerstone of his strategy. He had a market analysis made and segmented his market in a proper way.

He invested (during the loss year) some £15 million in marketing and on internal market-orientated activities, such as massive training in customer-service.

He had a new system designed to measure results on parameters that the local management really could influence, and he spent 60 per cent of his first year in the field, preaching his creed to all 24,000 employees.

After that first year the loss-maker showed a profit of some £50 million. And the second year some £60 million net profit.

Analysis

Strategy is, among other things, "What I want to get done in the long term". The long term is very variable. For Paul Wood, strategy was a question of installing the new layout whilst the production manager was on holiday. For Herbert Johnson and George Reid, strategy stretched five years ahead.

Derek Short's instinctive strategy was quite appropriate for an enterprise so dominated by his own personality.

John Clegg's strategy was based on identifying what his customers wanted, and on a great improvement in the service delivery system.

The time taken to decide a strategy is but a small fraction of the time and effort it takes to implement the strategy. It took only the time he was in his bath for Paul to work out how he would change the progress control system. It took him three weeks of sixteen hours a day to do the job – plus four months follow up before the new system was running smoothly.

Successful strategies are those which carry the commitment – the long-term commitment – of their sponsors. Paul was determined to see the job was done when many another person would have hidden behind the excuse of the production manager's delaying methods. Herbert tenaciously stood behind the profitability control concept for years.

Action Dos and Don'ts

DO
- Ask yourself where you want to be in the long term.
- Say how far away that is.
- Look at the chance you have of reaching your goal.
- If you want to change things, work out a simple statement of what.

DON'T
- Shoot for the moon.
- Try to make changes that are out of balance with the organisation – unless you have enough ammunition for a long war.

DO
- Stick to your strategies and see they succeed.

20 Target-setting

The successful manager is very tenacious of his strategy. He knows full well that any significant development always has to overcome obstacles – big obstacles – many of them unpredictable. Unless he sticks tenaciously and even fanatically to his strategy it will founder.

The setting of targets to be reached along the road is a help to him in implementing the strategy. Not rigid and inflexible targets, but mileposts on a path which could lead him towards success. These interim targets help in a variety of ways.

First they help him to concentrate on short-term activities which will lead in the right general direction. Without them he can too readily dissipate his effort.

Second, targets awaken people to opportunities which suddenly appear. The initiator alert for opportunities somehow seems to attract them. Luck works for him.

Third, a challenging target is a good motivator. It must, of course, be realistic. If somebody tells you that he expects you to perform in the next Olympic high-jump contest and win it, the likelihood that you would succeed even if you started practising today is minimal. Who could learn to jump 2.40 metres if he is completely unfit? The reverse is also true: if somebody tells you that he expects you to jump 50 cm next Spring, it seems stupid to start practising now. It is almost impossible for even an unfit person to fail at 50 cm.

If you want to change your jumping performance, you have to set your objectives at a reasonably high level, high enough to be a challenge but a challenge that it is possible for you to meet; and you have to set yourself interim targets for how, month by month, you will improve your performance.

Note that just stating that high-jumping is the game sensitises the person towards exercises that may increase the strength and flexibility of the legs. It is no use strengthening one's arm muscles, for instance.

Examples

Brian Lock and *Charles Farrow* were partners in separate firms of accountants, both successful and respected in their practices. At much the same time, when both were in their forties, they decided to break away from their respective partnerships and set up independent accountancy services.

Brian's strategy was to ensure a quick build-up of his practice. He priced his services at £100 per day and worked very hard for clients whom he had known from his earlier practice.

Charles' strategy was different. He priced his services at twice that much. He set out deliberately to build a prestige client list. He put a great deal of effort into building new contacts and into marketing his services. This left him less time for earning, but he was still able to equal Brian's turnover because of his higher rates.

After five years of independence, both were successful. Brian continued to be very busy, working mainly with the same clients and finding that one or two were dominating his activities. He regretted it, felt it was risky, but he was so busy working for them that he had neither the time nor very much desire to take other steps. He was captured in the routine of his daily work without the ability to develop his strategy.

Charles, on the other hand, had established a number of important clients locally, and had also come to the conclusion that he should spread his wings. His strategy was now to internationalise, and he set himself a target of establishing some work in America. He flew there to prospect for business.

When he was back home and at a client's office, mention was made of the lateness of returns from a small subsidiary company in Portugal.

Attending to both the client's needs and his own strategy of internationalising, Charles went to Portugal to improve the monthly accounting routines for his client. It was only a short assignment but he made other contacts there, and within twelve months found that he was going to Portugal for other clients once a quarter.

Now, five years further on still, Charles is very busy on the Iberian Peninsula, over there once a month. Indeed it has become a more important market for him than his home town area.

Brian in the meantime found his own activities focusing more and more on one client. Still trapped by his original strategy, he continued to work away until suddenly, in changed market conditions, his main client was taken over by a large group with their own professional accountancy staff. It was a grave blow for Brian and he needed to start rebuilding his practice.

Arthur Brown (we first met him in Chapter 2) was a committed strategist. Using the range of techniques of the strategic planners, he made far-reaching forecasts, set challenging strategies for the improvement of the company's profitability, and for the development of new markets and of new methods.

He recruited highly capable staff and with them prepared detailed plans for the development of the organisation in the future. The plans were most impressive. The planners were proud, committed, had a sense of mission together.

Their style of working was long-sighted, and they worked obsessively to implement their plans. So obsessively that they couldn't react quickly to changing conditions. Their strategy, systems, staff and visions were all focused on an expanding market. When the market changed, they couldn't cut back quickly enough, and their cash-flow problems were soon more serious than those of people who had planned far less.

People such as *Davey Jones*. Davey ran a printing works, a big printing house employing 400 people. Well established, products well known, equipment and technology stable. He was always proud of running a tight ship. He kept close to the market and in close touch with his customers.

Never one to go in for a lot of planning and cerebrating, Davey sensed the market setback, worried about it, stopped buying stocks and stopped replacing staff, and started a massive push for more business. In sensing and reacting to the situation, he was six months ahead of the more illustrious Arthur Brown, whose systems didn't clearly show the market situation for three months, and whose style (reviewing strategy and planning with frequent consultation) took another three months to implement.

Arthur had read all about pro-active management and did everything to put it into practice. Davey "didn't waste time on that sort of rubbish".

Davey was the man for the time.

Analysis

Whereas Brian Lock became trapped in his daily routine, Charles Farrow paid more attention to strategy and to setting himself challenging targets. The mission to America proved abortive. It didn't lead to him establishing business there. It did, however, make him sensitive to the possibilities in Portugal. When the opportunity arose, he was ready and anxious to grab it. He made luck work for him.

Great tenacity is needed to implement strategies; but it is no use unless blended with reasonable flexibility. Charles was flexible enough to switch from America to Iberia. Davey Jones reacted quickly to changing circumstances.

In deciding how to implement strategy, consider particularly whether you need to set targets for changing your systems, structure or skills:

- *Systems.* Do we need to change our system for planning, for control, for liaison?
- *Structure.* In what ways do we need to change our departmental organisation? What new appointments or what changes of responsibility for people? What consequent shuffling of responsibilities?
- *Skills.* In what ways must we build new abilities within our team?

The processes of management-by-objectives offer us a ready technique for target-setting:

- Define in general terms the priorities of the strategy: the key areas in which it is imperative that we produce results.
- Define for each area two or three specific actions needed to achieve the results. Define them as targets, in firm terms, measurable either in standards to be achieved or in target dates.
- Define the time at which progress towards the targets should be reviewed.

● At the review date, check and discuss progress and set new targets.

Action Dos and Don'ts

DO
● Think through the actions needed to implement your strategies.
● Set yourself challenging targets.
● Consult your staff and colleagues.
● Take action upstairs to enable you and your people to implement the strategy.

DON'T
● Overdo it.
● Become trapped by the system.

DO
● Be flexible and seize opportunities.

21 Shepherding

Think about the way the good shepherd keeps his flock moving.

Much as he might like to have them travel in a straight line and in a uniform pattern, he recognises that they will deviate a little, and he can see the pattern inside the flock constantly changing.

He doesn't worry about small deviations. He doesn't worry about the constantly changing internal pattern. What does concern him is that the general direction of movement should be in accordance with his strategy, and that any individuals straying far from the flock should be herded back in.

He doesn't always succeed, of course. The occasional sheep is lost and that causes a great deal of anxiety, but his key task is to keep the flock fit and progressing.

The manager has a similar shepherding role.

Examples

Per Alm is the benevolent autocrat whom we first met in Chapter 4: admired by most of his subordinates but feared and hated by a few. He is a strong leader and a strong supporter, not afraid of withering frankness. When people send him memos, he returns them signed with such comments as "Good work!", "Carry on!", "Drive hard!", or "Idiot!", "Stupid idea!" or "Have another go!". He is a great protectionist – if somebody tries to interfere with his people, that person is firmly put in his place.

John Clegg is the good guy who was appointed managing director of a company and rapidly turned it from a demoralised loss-maker into a confident profit-earner. Always charming and elegant, he can talk anybody's language. Starting with his view of the market situation and painting a bleak future for his company unless it changed, he soon signalled the sort of future he wanted to see. He is a strong believer that most people have far more talent than they are usually allowed to use – and he always seems to be right.

Jack Robinson was a factory manager. The factory's profits were adequate but never spectacular. His boss was an inspiring leader who suddenly discovered that Jack's wife was running a small business of her own which was selling ex-factory goods cheaply. There were some rather curious explanations and George had no hesitation. The good of the company was at stake and Jack had to go. He was out the same night.

Harold Ellis took over a factory which had been making traditional textiles. The equipment was elderly, the staff set in their ways, the system sketchy and the order and profit positions poor. It was a situation in which the company would not survive unless there were radical changes. It needed a new strategy for products, for processes, and for methods. It needed new systems. It needed a new vision and new attitudes.

There was no possibility of sudden radical change. Gradually, one step at a time, the organisation had to start moving in a new direction.

Analysis

These are all examples of shepherding.

Per Alm driving yet protecting.

John Clegg setting fresh visions and urging and helping his crew to move towards them.

Jack Robinson was the black sheep. He weakened the flock and had to be discarded by his shepherd.

Harold Ellis recognised that the flock could only be set moving initially at a relatively quiet pace – but the shepherd's job was to see that move started.

Action Dos and Don'ts

DO
- Be sure you know the direction you want the flock to go.
- Help them to keep moving that way.
- Give each a chance to use all his talents.
- Ensure that style, systems, structure and skills support your strategy and vision.

DON'T
- Worry about minor deviations.
- Interfere with the ever-changing informal pattern within your flock.

DO
- Act the good shepherd.

22 The Art of the Possible

The dedicated manager all too often meets frustrations. He is ulcer-prone. His dedication to producing satisfying results is such that he has a low tolerance for the difficulties and the hazards which surround any attempt at active managing.

Action is possible only as long as one concentrates on what is possible. Think about what you would like to do. Then think about what you can possibly do. Accept that some things are impossible.

Concentrate on the art of the possible.

The possible depends on the situation you are in. If you need a budget of £10,000 to introduce a new system and you've only got £1,000, then find out what you could achieve with £1,000. If it is not good enough, then the situation is impossible. Don't worry about it.

Similarly, if there are no markets whatever, if your existing procedures absolutely prohibit your course of action, if the organisation frustrates, or if the people are just not clever enough, then in each case it is impossible

186

to get things done. Stop worrying. Life is what it is.

It is not only situations which can prove impossible, it is also people.

There are conservative people, traditional people, self-interested people and many more, who will resist anything you want to do. Work on them, look for ways of manipulating them to your advantage; but if it is going to be impossible, accept the fact. People are what they are.

Not only "other people". I am what I am. It may be that I am seen to be awkward, pushful and for ever rocking the boat. No matter how hard I try to be nice and tolerant and responsible, it is a fact that I am seen to be awkward, pushful, rocking. At the end of the day I have to accept the fact. I am what I am. You are what you are. You have your own possibilities and your own limitations.

Accept that some things are possible and some impossible. Hope that some of the impossible may ripen into the possible. Seize every opportunity to help them to ripen; but, right now, concentrate on the best possible.

Work out the top priorities. Some will be to sustain the excellent performance of areas in which you are already succeeding, but others should be the best possible changes you can introduce. More about them in the next chapter.

Do not ignore your sales promotion. Make sure it is known and recognised that you are doing as excellent a job as it is possible for you to do.

Examples

Hans Jordan was plant manager at a factory within a large group. The factory made engines and employed 120 people. It worked on traditional lines, traditional layout, each man with his own job, MTM-based division of work.

Hans is a believer in people, in their urge to develop and their readiness to perform, given the right working conditions. However, the plant is embedded in a company culture where everybody knows "The Truth" and that truth is the way of working which has ruled for over twenty-five years. Hans accepted the way in which the group operated, regularly sent them the figures they asked for and kept them happy.

He accepted that it was impossible to change them, but he did not accept that it was impossible to change his own plant. He started discussions with his own people and with the shop stewards. Together they developed the idea of group organisation, i.e. a form of organisation where people as a group (normally five to nine people) have responsibility for a common output. How they divide the work between them is their business.

Hans and the shop stewards agreed that neither would inform their respective organisations of their plans. They agreed that it would be impossible to make progress if they did – there would be excessive interference. The art of the possible was to go ahead quietly.

Together with some staff in the plant, they developed a methodical plan for group organisation. This was welcomed by some people: others, more individualist or more conservative, were not ripe for such a change. Hans accepted the fact and let them carry on in the old way for the time being.

As the new organisation proceeded, it was easy to see positive results. People thrived. Production and quality went up. So did loyalty to the plant and to Hans.

Six months later, the individualists said that they too wanted group organisation. They have since become some of the most efficient and loyal members of Hans' team. It is now recognised as being the most efficient in the 5,000 people group, and has an overhead of only seven people instead of the standard twelve which it "ought" to have, according to Head Office.

We recently met Hans and his white-collar team, who had come away for a three-day working seminar. We asked him about productivity at the plant whilst he and the rest of the "bosses" were away, leaving it on its own. Hans mused for a moment and said that last time they were away for a week production went up by 7 per cent.

Bill Moss ran a production department employing sixty people. His materials came through a preparation department where twenty people were employed under *Jack Stubbs*.

Bill was unhappy about wastage. He believed that if test procedures could be changed in the preparation department, he would be able to reduce his own wastage record from 11 to 8 per cent. It would, of course, mean that the preparation people had to operate differently, but on balance would not mean more work for them.

Jack wasn't having any. He had run the preparation department for over twenty years and he wasn't proposing to change it at this stage.

Bill accepted that progress in that direction was going to be impossible until Jack retired in three years' time. Meanwhile Bill concentrated on the changes he could make within his own department, and did manage within the next two years to reduce wastage by 1½ per cent.

Ian Flood in his middle thirties was faced with a difficult work situation. He had been operating overseas for his company but came back home when it was appropriate for his children's education. Unfortunately he came home at a time of economic crisis and it was not easy for his company to find him a new role. Unfortunately, too, the person to whom he was made responsible was a pretty poor psychologist. He tucked Ian away in a non-job in an isolated office with little to do except stare at a blank wall and with firm instructions "not to worry". Ian worried. He began to feel that he might even be made redundant, and with far too much spare time he began to mope and lose the drive and enthusiasm he had shown while he was overseas.

After four months of this situation Ian was indeed made redundant. He was reasonably compensated, but now he was approaching his late thirties, jobless, in a difficult job market, despondent and dispirited. Everything seemed difficult. Life seemed oppressive. Fun was negligible. A great deal of help was needed before Ian was back on the rails.

Keith Jones was also made redundant at the same time, but he coped much better. As soon as he recognised that it was a possibility, he made a list of the things he could do to prevent it happening. Within the next couple of months, he worked through the list.

There was nothing more he could do to influence that situation. He accepted the fact and recognised that it would be a further four months before the situation was resolved, for better or for worse.

He set himself the task of using his spare moments during those four months to look after the interests of friends and allies who would miss him if he were to leave. Energetically Keith continued with his work and with the special side interest. He did not waste time moping about a situation he could do nothing about. When eventually he was made redundant, he channelled his still buoyant energy into the task of finding a new job, and had three job offers within ten days.

Analysis

Hans Jordan accepted the resistance to change from headquarters just as his shop stewards accepted there might be resistance from union officials. Hans accepted also that people are different, and did not try to force individualists to conform to the new organisation. He concentrated on the art of the possible.

Bill Moss had mental energy. He accepted that he would not make much progress with his quality control as long as Jack Stubbs stayed in charge of the preparation department. For Bill, the art of the possible was to concentrate on what savings he could achieve within his own four walls.

Ian Flood and Keith Jones illustrate typical problems when one is not able properly to use one's energy. Frustrated people turn inwards, mope, lose their thrust. To avoid such frustration you need to follow a four-point process:

1. Recognise what is frustrating you. You probably need to talk it through with somebody and to set it down as a simple short statement.
2. Analyse your options.
3. Accept that some things are beyond your influence.
4. Act on the possible.

Action Dos and Don'ts

DO
- Test everything you want to initiate: is it possible?
- Consider how it can be made possible.
- Try hard.
- Accept that some things are impossible for the moment.

DON'T
- Worry about the impossible.
- Worry without thinking whether it *is* possible.

DO
- Learn the art of the possible.

23 Changing Direction

One part of strategy is the ability to leave some things alone. That is the art of the possible.

Another part of strategy is to change matters.

What have you changed recently? Your planning system, your progress control, your organisation structure, the way you go about recruiting?

Whatever it was, you probably had to prepare the ground carefully, you had to overcome some resistance and you found some unexpected problems. If it was a major change, you probably had to give it your heavy commitment to overcome some of the snags.

That is the nature of change. It's tough.

Examples

Noel Blackburn's company had two key people in its sales force. *Colin Old* was the sales manager, mid-sixties,

masses of experience. *Barry Taylor* was the salesman/
assistant sales manager, thirty, well educated and technically qualified.

Colin spent his time sitting in his office, interminably
on the telephone. He rarely seemed to go out to see his
customers, and was showing signs of increasing age.

Noel wanted to relocate the sales office at his new
company headquarters, and it was natural that Colin
should retire rather than make the move to the new
location.

Barry was familiar with most of what Colin did, and
Colin gave him a full briefing before retiring.

The factory processes operated over a long cycle, nine
months from starting to make a product until ultimately it
was put into stock for sale, and much of the factory
ordering process seemed to have followed Colin's whims
and fancies. The managing director introduced a more
systematic ordering process, with stock records, production forecasts, sales records and sales forecasts. Monthly
the managing director met Barry and the production
manager to review and plan the orders to the factory.

It didn't work. Somehow, Colin's long telephone calls,
his sensitivity to what he heard and his years of
experience had led him instinctively to anticipate market
requirements nine months ahead. The more rational and
logical system could not compete. It caused costly chaos.

And the orders didn't come through the same. Under
Colin's system a customer would ring up and say: "We
need six months supply of 47 × 22s in a hurry", to which
Colin would reply: "Well now, we can let you have them
in six weeks. Is that good enough? And for your
purposes, wouldn't 17 × 21s do as well for the six weeks
in between?" But under the new regime Barry would set
out to visit the customer, though it might take ten days
before he could fit it into the schedule, and even then he
didn't know that the 17 × 21s would be a reasonable
alternative.

Factory ordering procedures and customer contacts
were just two of a dozen areas which had ticked along
adequately while Colin was there, but which were

exposed when he retired. There were difficulties with despatch, packaging, invoicing, debtors, quality requirements and waste disposal.

Just as soon as management started to change one of the processes, so another emerged into the limelight, needing urgent attention.

John Goldman's boss came in to see him one day. "I have been off to see the new subsidiary company, Jenkins', who came in six months ago", he said. "Tried to keep away from them so they would not feel we were breathing down their necks, but it really was time to hold out the hand of friendship and, by gum, John, it was clutched! They have over 100 per cent labour turnover from what I could make out from their figures, and the factory organisation looks like chaos.

"Old *Jack Jenkins*, their chairman, is convinced that it is all the fault of the local labour unions. So I put down a fiver, told him we could have his labour turnover down to 30 per cent and have the place ticking within twelve months: asked him to cover it. He did! How about it, John? How are you for time?"

During the next four weeks John was over at Jenkins' six times. He found things out, started setting new aspirations and generating enthusiasms. He helped the demoralised production manager to see new possibilities. He helped the supervisors, aroused their interest and keenness. He went to the canteen for an open meeting with the operatives. They responded desultorily, even pointing to the chipped and broken tray of crockery near John.

He picked up the tray, dropped it on the floor, smashed the lot, made a few choice comments and went to see Jack Jenkins and asked for £50 for new crockery. And got it.

The situation was now ripe for change. John helped to choose an operative who would become responsible for factory personnel and training matters, saw that she was properly trained and equipped, and arranged that she would have regular progress meetings with himself, the production manager and the senior supervisor.

Within four months, there was fresh enthusiasm and method. It was not all plain sailing – quite a few feathers were ruffled – but within twelve months both labour turnover and organisation structure were well under control. John went with his boss and Jack Jenkins, the production manager and the instructress, to spend the two £5 notes at the local bar.

Analysis

People grow accustomed to the established way of proceeding. When some small snag occurs in a well established system, people patch it up and it keeps running without too much trouble. But when one part of the system collapses or is put under severe stress, then all at once the faults elsewhere in the system become obvious. It is rather like turning over a stone on a rocky hillside on a nice sunny afternoon. Everything looks serene, but as the stone is turned over so a number of creepy-crawlies are revealed. They scatter. To catch them, another stone has to be turned and another horde of creepy-crawlies has to be chased.

That, in different terms, is what happened when Colin retired, taking with him the expertise and the intuition he had not even realised he was using.

Given such circumstances, Noel and his colleagues were under stress; the amount they could change at any time was limited and it became imperative for them to set out their priorities.

To make a success of changing things, there must be high commitment to them. Hence the emphasis we have placed in previous chapters on gaining commitment in establishing group goals and group strategies, and in group target setting.

And in waiting until the moment is ripe.

Togetherness, ripeness, momentum are essential ingredients for any change process, and must be cultivated.

When the time is ripe the change process takes five phases:

● Unfreeze.
● Enthuse.
● Create.
● Restructure.
● Refreeze.

Unfreeze. Think of the present situation as one which is frozen. It is iced up in people's routine procedures, their systems, their personalities, their relationships. Above all, in their attitudes.

The situation must be unfrozen. Somehow rouse conscious thought; recognise that action is now imperative. Bandy figures about. Talk about it in committees. Arrange a half-day conference, not to solve the problem, but to bring to people's attention that there is a problem. Break a tray of crockery if necessary. Then set out to analyse the problem. Try one of the problem-solving approaches described in Chapter 14.

Enthuse. Build people's sense of want for something to be done.

Create. Persuade people to agree what the problem really is, and what could be done about it.

"What will be done about it" is the *restructuring*. The new organisation's strategies, systems, staffs and skills. The new objectives, key result areas and targets.

There are bound to be snags and resistances. Any new method will be imperfect and will demand the precious enthusiasm, commitment and ripeness achieved at the outset. Always, there will be one or two particularly severe problems, which will stretch the commitment of the originators.

Finally, *refreeze*. Set up some means of keeping control and ensure that the new system continues to work.

Action Dos and Don'ts

DO
- Before you start trying to change anything, recognise that there will be unpredictable obstacles and resistance.
- In advance ensure that you build people's involvement and commitment.
- Wait for the moment to ripen.
- Unfreeze, enthuse and create before you start to restructure and refreeze.

DON'T
- Try to change too much too fast.
- Try to change before the time is ripe.

DO
- Commit yourself to make your change successful.

SUMMARY OF PART 4

This part of the book has been concerned with forces in the manager's balancing act which help him to steer his activities in the right direction.

"The right direction" must be a combination of his own personal goals and of realistic goals for his work-group.

Strategy is the grand design pointing in the right direction, implemented through targets on the route, accepting what is impossible to change or of low priority, and concentrating on what should and can be changed.

24 Balancing the Four Fields

The purpose of this book has been to offer a fresh way for busy people to exercise the art of managing.

The theme of the book has been the importance of keeping a balance between different activities. At the highest level, those activities have been described as in four main fields.

First, the field of making it a pleasure. This depends on the individual's character in some ways which are deep set, and it depends also on the more controllable job of stating expectations, challenging but realistic. It depends on relationships with friends, allies and enemies; it depends on the culture of the company in which one works; and inevitably, the intensity of a manager's work-life spills over to affect his private life. Part 1 of the book dealt with those aspects of enjoying managing, and making it Fun.

Results became the theme in Part 2. This was treated as the manager's need himself to do things, with his manager's task being to ensure that things were done.

This took us into the areas of organising, knowing what ought to be done, delegating, inspiring, acting as a catalyst and developing people. It required control systems and it needed positive thinking. Together, these forces form a battery of tools to produce Results.

Part 3 focused on the manager's position, his need to Achieve the Ability to influence his surroundings and to control his own effectiveness. Forces discussed in this part were having the chance to perform, relating to surroundings and colleagues, and improving one's position. There was a series of tips on self-organisation and personal skills, and on the need to adapt to one's "customers".

Finally, in Part 4 we have switched to making sure that effort is expended in a sensible Direction. This has to take account of personal goals and of group goals which lead to strategy and to methods of implementing strategy.

So we leave with two final suggestions for making the most out of this book. The first is to draw a cross and put at the end of each arm the four key areas.

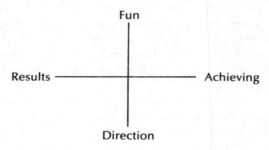

Now mark off along each arm some distance from the centre which will show your satisfaction and success in that field. Do you find a well balanced picture? What implications are there for your own action?

Finally, this book has introduced you, using anecdotes, to a number of our friends. Try writing one anecdote about yourself as a dissatisfied manager and two as a satisfied manager.

Appendix: Note on Sources

This appendix is intended for the reader concerned to check on our sources and perhaps add to his reading list.

Most of the material in the book is based on our personal experience, and is presented in a form which is our original thinking. It owes much to our contacts with friends in the business world, and to the practices, good and bad, which we have picked up from them.

It is also based on what we think is an educated acquaintance with management literature. We perceive that literature as forming a series of streams: for example, the organisational structuralists from Fayol to Urwick and beyond; the system writers both from the work-study fields and from the planning fields, such as Ansoff; and the behaviouralists from MacGregor to Maslow, Herzberg, Likert, Vroom and company. Each of these streams of thought has influenced us and is compounded into the elementary frameworks used within the book.

Some authorities are used more directly within the

book. Below on a chapter by chapter basis we acknow-
ledge them to the best of our ability.

The general concept of balancing fields is our own.

In Chapter 2, "Having the Urge", we used David
McClelland's concepts of motivation from *The Achieving
Society* (1960).

Chapter 3, "Friends, Allies and Enemies", uses very
general concepts from games theory, as introduced by
Jacobo A. Varela in his *Psychological Solutions to Social
Problems* (Academic Press, 1971).

Chapter 4, "Company Culture" is based on raw
material from, among others, Deal and Kennedy's *Corporate Culture* (1983).

Chapter 5, "Private Lives", comprises mainly our own
thinking, but we were first introduced to the idea of
discriminating between work/self/family forces by Colin
Sheppard of Sheppard Moscow Associates. Chapter 6,
"Doing Things", is also our own thinking.

Chapter 7, "Getting Things Done", starts with a
description of the Indevo Consultancy Group's Trim
model. The concept in Section 7B of the Time Span of
Discretion goes back to Elliot Jacques and his book *The
Changing Culture of a Factory*. In the same section we
use the "Why/What/How" hierarchy, to which we were
first introduced by Bob Miller of Harold Whitehead and
Partners. Section 7C, "Organising", as originally drafted,
was a major chapter, drawing on a host of writers on the
subject. However, that chapter is appropriate for a more
general book on management; for this book, intended
for the individual manager, we have restricted ourselves
to a short treatment, which as far as we know is original.

Section D in Chapter 7, "Inspiring", is original, but
strongly influenced by the various products of the
Nederlands Paedagogisch Instituut. The final two sections of Chapter 7 are original thinking. So is Chapter 8.

The sources for Chapter 9, "Positive Thinking",
obviously include the writings of Edward de Bono, even
though they are not used in any explicit way.

Chapter 10, "The Chance to Perform"; Chapter 11,

"Timing"; and Chapter 12, "Colleagues"; are our own thinking.

The framework used in Chapter 13, "Improving One's Position", draws heavily on the ideas of Phillip Marsh of Leeds University, Department of Management Studies. We have used private communications as the basis for the chapter. More detail can be found in the following: Hickson *et al.* "A Strategic Contingencies Theory of Intra-organisational Power", *Administrative Science Quarterly*, 1971, pp. 216–29; Mechanic, D. "Sources of Power of Lower Participants in Complex Organisations", *Administrative Science Quarterly*, 1962, pp. 349–64; and Minzberg, H. *Power is Around Organisations*, Prentice-Hall, 1983.

Chapter 14, "Self-organisation" is based on our own thinking, spiced with William Reddin's thinking; with Zero Base Budgeting theory, and a problem solving model ("Force Field Analysis") to which we were introduced by Colin Sheppard.

Chapter 15, "Personal Skills", draws on private communication with Barrie Hopson, Life Skills Associates, Leeds. It includes also a fragment from Bill Scott's *Communication for Professional Engineers* (Thomas Telford, 1984).

Chapter 16, "Adapting to One's Customers", is based on Richard Norman's book *Service Management* (Liber, 1982).

The framework in Chapter 17, "Personal Goals", draws heavily on private communications with Helmuth J. ten Siethoff, Nederlands Paedagogisch Instituut.

In Chapter 18, "Group Goals", we use Thomas J. Peters' and Robert Waterman's book *In Search of Excellence* (1983).

The framework in Chapter 19, "Strategy", is based on our own experience.

Chapter 20, "Target-setting", uses main-stream general management, spiced with a little Peters and Waterman and a good deal of John Humble's *Management by Objectives*.

The idea of Chapter 21, "Shepherding", was prompted

by Peters and Waterman, *op. cit.*, but the treatment is original.

Chapter 22, "The Art of the Possible", is original.

Chapter 23, "Changing Direction", draws on change theory from the Tavistock Institute for Human Relations, and the writings of various authors there.

Chapter 24, "Balancing the Four Fields", takes us back to Square One.